A MAN OF T...

RECOLLECTIONS

OF

WARREN V. KELLER, A NEBRASKAN

As Told To

Rosemarie Keller Skaine

and

James C. Skaine

with a foreword by John Douglas Russell

Author's Castle, Publisher
Cedar Falls, Iowa

Cover: Warren V. Keller, 1926

Library of Congress Cataloguing-in-Publication Data

Library of Congress Catalog Card Number: 99-90634

Keller, Warren V.
Skaine, Rosemarie Keller
Skaine, James C.
    A Man of the Twentieth Century: Recollections of Warren V. Keller, A Nebraskan as Told to Rosemarie Keller Skaine and James C. Skaine / by Warren V. Keller, Rosemarie Keller Skaine, and James C. Skaine; with a foreword by John Douglas Russell.
        p.   cm.
    Includes index.
    ISBN 0-9672240-0-4 (Perfect Bound softcover: 60# paper)
    1. Biography / Autobiography / Letters 2. Family / Relationships 3. History - Nebraska

©1999 Warren V. Keller, Rosemarie Keller Skaine, James C. Skaine. All rights reserved.

No part of this book may be reproduced or transmitted in any form or by any means, electronic or mechanical, including photocopying or recording, or by any information storage and retrieval system, without permission in writing from the publisher.

Manufactured in the United States of America.

Author's Castle, Publisher
P.O. Box 1044, Cedar Falls, IA 50613

Printed by
RECORD PRINTING COMPANY
CAIRO - NEBRASKA

In memory of the lives of love they lived

Marie W. Kuehner Keller, wife
William H. Keller, son
Rose A. Jinks Keller. mother
Harvey S. Keller, father

Acknowledgments

Generous thanks to Dad, Warren V. Keller, Grand Island, Nebraska, for his tireless cooperation and expansive knowledge of the 20th century. Most of all we thank him for his unconditional love.

Many thanks to Ruby Burnett Schoel Loop, Grand Island, Warren's lady-friend, for her participation in *A Man of the Twentieth Century*, and for her enthusiastic spirit.

We thank Robert Kramer, Professor Emeritus, Center for Social and Behavioral Research and Department of Sociology, Anthropology, and Criminology for his assistance in computer technology and programs. Bob's generous giving of his knowledge and time enabled us to produce this book more quickly and so much better than it could have been otherwise.

Special appreciation is extended to Pastor John Russell, St. Pauls Lutheran Church, Grand Island for his ministry to Warren over the years and for writing the foreword.

We thank John and Rosie Whyte, Warren's neighbors, for their support and who, at a critical moment, made a life-saving difference for Warren.

We thank Warren's former neighbors, Howard Maxon, Emergency Management Director for Grand Island-Hall County, and his wife, Colleen Maxon, a secretary for the City of Grand Island Building Inspection Department, for their many good deeds to Warren, and the Maxon children, John Howard, Paul Andrew, and Luke Adrian, for the love and company they freely give to Warren.

Special thanks to Nebraska relatives who love Warren and gave emotional and intellectual support for *A Man of the Twentieth Century*; in particular Richard L. and Nancy L. Kuehner, Phillips, and William V. and Carolyn E. Guenther Kuehner, Doniphan, Rosemarie's cousins, for reading drafts and providing good ideas. We thank also the children of William V. and Carolyn E. Guenther Kuehner: Karla K. Kuehner Obermeier, her husband Jackie L. Obermeier and their son, Tanner William Obermeier, Kaila K. Kuehner, Kenda K. Kuehner and William E. Kuehner, II and his wife, Jennie Akerlund Kuehner. Their many kindnesses extended to Warren are deeply appreciated.

Thanks to Fred H. Bosselman, Rosemarie's cousin, and his wife, Maxine Forbes Bosselman, Grand Island, for encouragement and shared book experiences. Mr. Bosselman's book, *A Man from Worms* by William F. Arendt, Record Printing Company, Cairo, Nebraska, 1994 and Mrs. Bosselman's cook book, *The*

Acknowledgments vii

Bosselman Family & Friends Cookbook, 1997, Morris Press, Kearney, Nebraska, were excellent examples to follow.

We thank the children of Ruby Loop, Dorothy Schoel Baker, Wills Point, Texas, Monadine Schoel Dubas and Marceline Schoel Forst and her husband, Donald Forst, Grand Island, and Ercel Schoel and his wife, Bernelda Poehler Schoel, Afton, Oklahoma, for their love freely given to Warren.

Thanks to Lucille Sloggett Goehring, Grand Island, cousin, for her willingness to answer many questions pertaining to this book and for her love.

We appreciate the generous help of Leslie A. Vollnogle, Assistant Curator, Stuhr Museum, Grand Island, in selecting photographs and Joan Cox, Librarian, Mason City, in researching Keller family history.

We appreciate our friend in Cedar Falls, Iowa, Rosemary Miller, for reading drafts of this book.

Our appreciation goes to Robert R. Hardman, Professor and Director, Information Technology Services (ITS)- Training Services, Darrell G. Fremont, Coordinator of Multimedia Development, and Betty M. Johnson, Office Coordinator; and the students and staff at ITS-User Services, Computer Consulting Center, at the University of Northern Iowa, Cedar Falls, for their assistance with the reproduction of graphics.

We thank Tim Mohanna and the staff of Record Printing Company, Cairo, Nebraska, for their excellent workmanship and the way they facilitated the printing of this book.

We thank the church members of St. Pauls Lutheran Church who befriended Warren, in particular Eloise Sherry and Mrs. Elsie Hendrickson from Cairo who gave him rides to The Stephen's Ministry in the Spring of 1995.

Heartfelt thanks to Todd Skaine, Minneapolis, Minnesota, Warren's grandson, and James Taylor Jeremiah, "T.J." Skaine, Warren's great grandson, for their love.

Rosemarie Keller Skaine
James Cole Skaine

Table of Contents

Acknowledgments — v

Foreword by Pastor John Russell — xi

Preface by Rosemarie Keller Skaine — xiii

Preface by James C. Skaine — xv

Introduction — 1

Chapter

1. 1900-1909 — 7
2. 1910-1919 — 17
3. 1920-1929 — 29
4. 1930-1939 — 39
5. 1940-1949 — 49
6. 1950-1959 — 63
7. 1960-1969 — 71
8. 1970-1979 — 77

9.	1980-1989	85
10.	1990-1999	97
Appendix		*117*
Index		*129*

Foreword

Unique. Perhaps this is the best word I can think of to describe Warren Keller. He is a unique man in so many ways. No, he did not achieve greatness according to the standards of this world. He did not rise to positions of greatness in the business world. Nor did he amass great wealth as a result of fantastic business ventures.

John Russell, Pastor, St. Pauls Lutheran, Grand Island, Nebraska

In his own special way he is unique. Born nearly a hundred years ago, it was necessary for him to join the work force when he was a young boy and he stayed in the work force until he was eighty-three years old - long after most people not only stopped work but stopped living as well. This says something about his determination to always explore new opportunities and to be open to new possibilities.

What person would sign up for an eight month class in their 96th year except Warren, a class which included taking on ministry responsibilities when it was over? Now, at 99, he can be seen wheeling the "old people" around in their wheelchairs at Wedgewood - his daily afternoon "ministry" responsibility as a Stephen Minister. And what person at 99 attends worship services 51 times during 1998 except Warren?

This is why I say he is unique. He stands out with special qualities that we all have come to admire at St. Pauls. He serves to remind all of us that there are always new opportunities and possibilities for us to explore. As long as we are alive, he reminds us, we need to be exploring these opportunities which can give quality to our lives. He truly understands with the Lord there is no retirement program. At every age there are ways in which we can ministry and do the Lord's work. If only other people could learn the lesson he learned, to learn from his example.

Today we celebrate with this publication a very unique and special person.

Pastor John Douglas Russell
St. Pauls Lutheran Church
Grand Island, Nebraska

Preface

From Horses to Space Shuttles

To write recollections of my near centenarian father, Warren V. Keller, a native Nebraskan, has been a long standing desire of mine. Born in 1900, Dad's life spans the twentieth century. He has seen a lot of change. It is my hope to capture some of the Century's changes along with some of my father's reactions to those changes. Dad always has had the ability to meet and accept change in a positive manner, but in his heart, his loyalty is to the early years of the 20th century. Things were simpler then, he often says, adding, "This is not my world." Yet, when I sought wisdom and comfort to understand my own conflictive views about a changing world, Dad, as fathers do, took my mind by the hand and led the way to accept change. Dad is a timeless treasure.

The book is divided by decades for ease of identifying the time frame and to assist in understanding my father's life. His story, a great story, of a courageous, loving son, husband, father and grandfather needs to be preserved for those of us that follow his footsteps, but will never be able to fill their generosity of spirit.

His humanity will live forever in the hearts of all who know him.

Rosemarie Keller Skaine

Preface

The Themes of a Rich Life

In 1955, when I first met Dad Keller, I was a college student and was dating his daughter. I was impressed with him and with his ability to make a rich, active life for himself and his family.

Over the years, I have enjoyed listening as he retold stories of his life. He told me of the time he saw his first car, of living by the railroad in Mason City, Nebraska, of working on the bridge gang, of coming to Grand Island to live, of working for the City, of building his house on West 16th Street, of the weather and how it affected his life, of traveling throughout the country, of keeping his house and cars in good working order, of the people he met and helped as he worked for the city, and of his family and church.

Dad Keller is a true son of Nebraska and of the 20th Century. Interwoven themes run through his life and define his existence. He has an abiding love for cars and other technological marvels that were new in this century and he appreciated the challenges and rewards they give. He had a strong heritage in building -- building bridges, his house, a strong family, a strong faith and relationships. He watched the roads change from barely identifiable trails to modern superhighways and he loved to travel them.

Dad does not have a formal education beyond the 10th grade, but I have always said that he is one of the best educated people I know. He has learned from life and has passed that knowledge on to those around him. He was a teacher for me. He inspired me.

I have known Dad for less than half of his life, but through the stories he shared with me over the years, I feel I have known him and experienced his world throughout all of the 20th Century. I am pleased and proud to be part of these Recollections.

James Cole Skaine

Introduction

Heritage[1]

I was born of families that came to America early in our country's history. My mother's family, the Amsberrys were related to Richard Everett, who came from England on the Mayflower in 1620. My dad's family, the Kellers, came to Philadelphia in 1752.

The Pilgrims landed at Plymouth in 1620 in the Massachusetts Bay Colony. Richard Everett, one of the earliest settlers, was a forefather of Polly Everett, wife of William Amsberry. Polly and William gave birth to Francis Everett Amsberry on January 18, 1824, in Southside, West Virginia. Francis married Lucy Beard Amsberry (1827-1915). On March 4, 1885, Francis and Lucy left for Nebraska by renting a freight railroad car, 60' x 10'. Francis homesteaded until his death, August 6, 1897, in Mason City, Nebraska.

My grandmother, Margaret Amsberry Jinks, was one of Francis and Lucy's 12 children. She married William Robert Jinks(1848-1888) and they had four children. My mother, Rose A. Jinks, was born September 16, 1874, in Southside, West Virginia. Her father died of tuberculosis in 1888 and was buried at the Viers Chapel Cemetery at Southside. My grandmother Margaret took her four children and moved to Mason City, Nebraska in 1889. In 1896, Grandmother Margaret married Nikolai Peterson (1852-1923) of Mason City.

Amos Keller, writer of the *Henry Keller Genealogy*, visited Switzerland in 1903 and found a marble slab in the basement of the Minstral Cathedral in Basel with the following inscription: "Jacob Keller, the butcher, died Oct. 13, 1572." In Professor I.D. Rupp's "30,000 Immigrants," Dr. S. Shumaker found 56 inscriptions with the name of Keller who came to Pennsylvania from Switzerland, from the Palatinate and other parts of Germany. Although some Kellers can be placed in Bavaria, family historians believe that the plague in the fourteenth century caused many ancestors to move down from the mountains into the Rhine countries to escape the "Black Death." The famous Rhine has its sources in the Alps, the Keller family has its sources in the country of Tell and Zwingli. The Kellers' Swiss ancestors had much in common with people in Germany and often married or had like religious ties in Europe and thus came to America with a common desire for a peaceful home in a new world. P. S. Rhodes, associate historian, Woodstock, Virginia, Shenandoah County, Virginia found at least three distinct families that located in the country before the Revolution.

The Hottel Shield

Introduction

My father was Harvey S. Keller who was born October 20, 1868 in New Amsterdam, Indiana to John M. Keller (1836-1912) and Jane Weaver Keller (1842-1923). My father was a seventh generation direct descendant of John Hottel, a Swiss immigrant who came to Port Philadelphia, Pennsylvania on September 11, 1732. Barbara Anna Hottel, born in Europe about 1730, married George Keller after arriving in Pennsyl-

Back row left to right: Etna, Lorena, me, Blanche ; Front row left to right: Emery, my father Harvey, Twila, my mother Rose, and Clara

vania. Historians estimate that George was born in Schwarzenacker, near the city of Zweibrucken, Bavaria because his younger brother, Joseph Keller, was born there on March 15, 1719. Founded in the 1750s, the Keller homestead stands today in Mt. Olive just outside of Toms Brook, Virginia. In 1994, I visited Tom's Brook and also went to Southside, West Virginia and Amsterdam, Indiana. I had always wanted to visit my roots. In 1995, I again went to Southside and attended the Hottel-Keller reunion.

I was one of seven children born to Harvey and Rose I was born in Mason City, Nebraska, on January 29, 1900. I had five sisters and one brother. They are:
> Lorena (November 9, 1896 - July 10, 1983) who married Wayne Coxen on August 23, 1917 in Mason City.
>
> Blanche (June 25, 1898 - December 28, 1985) who married Frank Edwards on October 25, 1920 in Mason City.
>
> Etna (November 11, 1902 - September 1, 1953) who married Juan Sloggett on June 22, 1923.
>
> Clara (April 8, 1907 - June 1, 1962) married Lewis Roberts on November 26, 1925 at her parents's home, 1204 W. 9th in Grand Island. Her second marriage was to Henry Allen on May 26, 1960.
>
> Emery (March 10, 1910 - April 28, 1969) married Margaret Evans on Sept. 17, 1929 in the Grand Island Court House. Emery had two other marriages.
>
> Twila (August 31, 1912 - April 12, 1993) who

Introduction

married Wallace Densmore on April 19, 1933 at her parents's home, 1204 W. 9th in Grand Island.

My mother died on April 11, 1958 and my dad died August 29, 1959. Both are buried at Hillsboro, Oregon.

I married Marie W. Kuehner (1905-1979) of Doniphan, Nebraska on December 23, 1926. Together we lived for 52½ years in Grand Island, Nebraska. Marie died on May 31, 1979. My son, Bill, (we named him William Henry) was born on August 15, 1930. He died on July 19, 1980.

My daughter, Rosemarie, was born on June 11, 1936. She married Jim (James Cole Skaine) on June 4, 1957. Jim was born on January 3, 1936 in Monongahela, Pennsylvania. Rosemarie and Jim gave me three grandchildren: James Keller Skaine (1961-), Camille Marie Skaine (1962-1964), and Forrest Todd Skaine (1965-). All of them were born in Ithaca, New York. I have three great grandchildren: Melissa Keller and James Keller, adopted by James Keller Skaine *a.k.a.* James Keller and Carin Little Keller, (1959 -), and James Taylor Jeremiah Skaine (1997-) born to Todd and Alecia Cleve (1973-).

This is a brief look at my heritage.

ENDNOTES

1. Ruby Roberts Coleman, Compiler, *The William A. Amsberry (Amsbary) and Related Families*, 1002 Highland Dr., Ogallala, Nebraska, 1970, 113pp; *History of the Descendants of John Hottel*, Shenandoah Publishing House, Inc., Strasburg, Virginia, 1930, introduction of "Barbara Hottel," 820-821, 1044-1047; Amos Keller of Tiffin, Ohio and Rev. E. S. Shumaker, D.D., Indianapolis, Indiana, *Henry Keller Genealogy*.

Chapter 1
1900-1909

Born at the Turn of the Century

When you come to think of it, I almost was never born because of what nearly happened to my mother and father on their wedding day. My parents were married on April 2, 1894 in Broken Bow, Nebraska. Uncle Jess and Aunt Becky Amsberry stood up with them. On the way back, the dust and wind blew so hard, they could hardly see anything. At one point, the horses stopped and wouldn't go. They got out to see

Mason City, Nebraska, 1900

why, and a train sped by. The horses saved their lives.

It was a cold day when I was born on January 29 in 1900. I was born in a one room sod house in Mason City, Nebraska. Mason City was founded in 1886 by the Lincoln Land Company who purchased it from homesteaders, Nels Anderson and Mrs. George Runyan.

Mason City was named after Honorable O.P. Mason, formerly a Supreme Court Judge for Nebraska Territory. Its first post office was established in 1886.[1]

When I was born, I had two sisters, Lorena and Blanche. We lived in Mason City for a while, then moved to Ashland, Nebraska for a short time and then back to Mason City. When I was two, the family moved again, this time to Edison, Washington. We went to Washington on a train and came back on a train. Edison was a little town outside Seattle, where my dad worked at a sawmill.

I remember one Fourth of July, a circus was in town. My Uncle Burt Amsberry told me I could have a sack of peanuts or go to the circus. I took the peanuts.

We came back to Mason City soon after my sister Etna was born. I am not sure why we came back, but I was told that my Grandma Peterson said that she wouldn't speak to my mother again if they didn't come back and show her my sister, Etna. Etna was born in Washington. She was the only one of my sisters and brothers who was not born in Nebraska. We lived in Edison for about a year and a half.

Warren at one year

Chapter 1 - 1900-1909

When we came back to Mason City, we lived in

Warren V. Keller's 1904 sod home, located 1 ½ miles north of Mason City, Nebraska

a two-room sod house located in the country 1 ½ miles north of town. It didn't have any floors and didn't leak when it didn't rain. One day, I remember watching my mother sprinkle water over the dirt floor to settle the dust in the family bedroom. The beds rested on boards so they wouldn't sink into the ground. The closest water supply was 100 feet from the house.[2] We had no convenience at all. We had a pump outside and a little coal oil lamp.

My dad raised a garden and he'd walk to town and get whatever work he could find, maybe work for the butcher and get a little meat for us to eat. We lived there in the sod house for a while, and then we moved into town where Dad worked at odd jobs from then on. When my Dad worked on a thresher machine, he and the others just slept under the machine. This he did at about the time we came to town.

When I was five years old, I started to school in Mason City. When I first went to school, I started in chart class, that's what they called it in those days instead of kindergarten. And I went to school like any other kid. Soon, we changed school buildings. We moved around on another hill to a cement block school house that they had just built. I went to school there for the rest of my school years.

I had about three blocks to go to school, and our folks would dress us up with plenty of clothes. We walked to school. They never took us to school. We'd waller around through the snow drifts. If there was a snow drift across the road or anywhere else, it stayed there until it thawed in the spring, because there weren't any cars. People would just walk or drive their horses over or around the drifts, and that's the way they got around 'til spring came and it was all thawed out and the mud had dried up. Even if it was blizzarding, the folks paid no attention. They just dressed us and we walked to school. And that's the way things were until it thawed out in the spring.

Around home I was like any other kid, I helped plant the garden and get the eggs. At night I'd get a coal oil lamp and get the bugs off the potatoes. We'd have to make our own toys for play.

My folks had no education and they did what they thought was right. They lived and let live. My mother was a kind and religious woman who loved and

Chapter 1 - 1900-1909

was loved by everyone. My dad was a quiet man and said little. He was a quiet man who lived by the Bible.

There was no conversation at the table. My folks never said anything unless they wanted us kids to do something. We didn't say no. Mom read the Bible and visited the neighbors. Dad worked 12 hour days. One time, Dad bought a big elm tree for $1.00 and we talked about the tree and his work.

When I was a boy, the kids in the family always ate last. We had to wait. I would get awful headaches because I had to wait. I never had to cook or do a dish; those were my sisters' jobs.

My sisters played together, but my only brother, Emery, didn't come along until I was 10 years old. So, I was a loner. I didn't know what or who I was.

Grandmother Maggie Peterson used to wring her hands when a storm was coming. It wasn't until I knew who I was that I overcame my own fear. I respect lightning, but I'm not scared.

I was a bashful kid. I never ask anyone for anything. I got it on my own, and learned a lot in a little bit.

My Dad moved from one house to another a lot. I don't know why, but it made me not want to move again. Dad always chose a house on flat land. I would have loved to live in a house on the side of a hill. After the sod houses, we lived in seven frame houses and one cement block house all within a range of five or six blocks. The frame houses were pretty good sized houses, but they were drafty and sometimes cold.

On some cold winter days when we lived in the frame houses, I tried to obey my mother by washing my face before breakfast. I sometimes discovered the water surface in the basin was covered with an inch or two of ice. We'd have to thaw the dipper out. This was our drinking water, so we'd pour some into the wash basin, wash ourselves with our hands because there were no wash cloths. We dried our hands on a towel, but it wasn't a Turkish towel like we have now. Our hands were usually wet, even when we dried them. Then when we were finished washing, we'd throw the water out the back door. If the house had a porch, we'd go outside and throw it past the porch.

We also had a large reservoir of water that set to the back of the stove, down the side of the oven, and level with the stove. It held around 10 to 15 gallons. At night just before my Dad would go to bed, he would shake all the ashes out of the stove to let it cool. Then he'd put some paper, kindling and coal in it so that in the morning all he would have to do was light the stove with a match. The volume of water in the reservoir kept the water from freezing and also kept the stove warm. Oh, there might be a thin layer of ice, but nothing very thick. We always had water from this tank if we wanted it.

'Course we had to run to the alley to use the privy. We didn't have toilet paper. Most Sears & Roebuck or Montgomery Ward catalogues ended up in

Chapter 1 - 1900-1909

the privy. The privy had two seat holes, one large and one small. When the dirt hole filled up, we'd dig a new hole next to it, throw the dirt from the new hole over the old hole, then set the privy over the new hole.

In one frame house, I had a bedroom right by the railroad tracks. We'd find small nails to put on the tracks, and the trains would flatten them as they passed by. We just did anything to pass away the time. A couple of times, I rode with the engineer.

Most mail came in the morning, and that is when you would see everyone, around nine. Most people would get their mail and then they'd go home and eat breakfast. They'd have dinner around 3 o'clock. But we had three meals a day. We never had snacks. We had breakfast at six in the morning, dinner at 12 noon, and supper at six in the evening.

I was 8 years old when I first saw store baked bread. It came from Gooch's in Lincoln. The train came up in the morning and went back in the afternoon. My bedroom was on the side of the house by the tracks. The Burlington train traveled on them.

Dad worked with a dray wagon for a while. They would hire out to haul or move merchandise, and take the cream from creamery to the depot, or merchandise to the store. They'd haul sand for cement if someone was going to build a house. Whatever came in on the trains, Dad had to deliver to the stores. He'd work ten hours a day in addition to caring for the horses before the day began and after the ten hours were over.

I did not see my first car until I was nine. It was an old Rambler with a two cylinder engine crossways. You had to crank it on the side. It didn't have anything but a buggy seat, no top or sides. You guided it with a lever instead of a wheel. It would probably go 15 miles an hour if that fast. The wheels were about the size of a buggy wheel. I grew to love cars and loved to travel in them.

I stayed at home all year round until I was about seven years old. Then I would stay with my Granddad Peterson or my Uncle Roberts out on the farm on Saturdays and in the summer time. I never went into town much, because we didn't have any money to blow. I stayed at my grandparents out on the farm until I was 12 years old. The farms were so far apart that there never were any children to play with, so I was pretty much by myself all the time. I never played any sports. I lived among the meadow larks, coyotes and rabbits. So, I never really knew what was going on very much. We never got any paper because nobody ever ordered any. I helped my Grandfather Keller deliver his vegetables and stuff he sold, and just passed away the time until I was about seven years old.

I only remember asking two questions of my Dad when I was in school, and both times his answers were wrong. One, I asked him how far it was to the end of the world? and he said, "There wasn't any end." Then I asked him what other movement the sun had besides going around the earth? He told me, "The sun just kind

Chapter 1 - 1900-1909

of rocked back and forth." I didn't ask him questions like these again.

My parents were good people. I never heard them quarrel. My mother was a quiet religious woman. She never advised me about anything. I guess she left that to Dad, who hardly ever talked. So what I learned, I learned on my own, picking up things here and there.

The first church I went to was an old sod chicken house. We sat on nail kegs on a plank. We didn't have any preacher. Whoever preached was a hard shell Baptist. He'd chew tobacco and spit. People couldn't read. We'd listen to the preacher about hell and damnation and sing a couple songs. So, people back then would pick a couple verses from the Bible and live by them.

My folks rested on Sunday and didn't go to church much. Dad worked 12 hours a day, 6 days a week. They needed to rest.

One day, Granddad Peterson turned something upside down that looked like a creamery can. I didn't know what it was. It played "Drakes" and "Turkey in the Straw," "A Forage in the Forest," and "Shuffling off to Buffalo." It was a Victrola.

When I was a kid and someone died, the dead got to ride in a hearse with rubber wheels, but if you were attending the funeral, you had to ride in a wooden wagon with wooden wheels. Now, why do you suppose that's the way it was?

ENDNOTES

1. *Mason City 1886-1976*, A Bicentennial Project, 1976, Loup Valley Queen, Callaway, NE, 3, 4.

2. *Mason City 1886-1976*, A Bicentennial Project, 1976, Loup Valley Queen, Callaway, NE, 3, 4.

Chapter 2
1910-1919

A Life of Work as a Teen

Main Street, Mason City, 1911

During the summers of 1912 and 1913, I worked as a hired hand on the Chester Lamb farm outside Mason City. Chester was not kin folk, but I did have relatives in Mason City named Lamb. Chester and his wife had eight or ten kids, but they had four when I was working there, Leonard, Leah, Mabel and Carey. Leonard was about my age. I didn't have much contact with anyone except with the family at mealtimes.

It was a lonely job. The jackrabbits and birds were my companions during the long days of doing chores and working in the fields.

I got up at about 4:00 in the morning, went to the pasture to get the horses, then harnessed 12 head of horses and milked seven cows, took care of the hogs, and separated the milk and did the rest of the chores. Then I'd eat breakfast and I'd go to the field and work for 10 hours walking behind horse-drawn machinery. I had an hour off for noon. Then, I'd go back to the house at night and we'd have supper. And then I'd go take care of the horses. I'd do all the same chores over again. I'd get to bed about 10:30 - 11:00. I did that for the two summers for 50 cents a day, sun up to sun down. I never saw the 50 cents. It must have gone directly to Dad.

Most of the time I was on the farm. But, when I was 10 or 12, I cleaned a corner lot for the banker in Mason City. I expected at least a quarter, but I got 15 cents.

Other kids had money, and I wondered why I didn't get some money. My Mom skimped and saved so that we could take a penny to Sunday School, and every 4th of July I'd get a nickel. I had to decide between the merry-go-round and pop. It wasn't until I was 16 that I chose a can of pop. It was lemon. There was no other money until Christmas. Sometimes I would mix corn candy and peanuts, but basically I grew up without any money.

We kids would pick wild berries and choke cherries. We'd get them along the road in the canyon by Aunt Priscilla Caldwell's farm. We'd get corn shucks from farmers for our mattresses. My Dad's dad had ten tame cherry trees in his back yard, and I'd have to go pick the cherries. He sold garden stuff to people,

Chapter 2 - 1910-1919

and I took my little wagon and took it around to people.

My Dad's dad was buried on my birthday in 1912. He was 72 years old, and everyone thought he was an old man, and a nice old man. Nowadays, that's not considered so old.

When I was around 11 or 12 years old, just before Twila was born, we lived in a cement block

My Burro and Me at the Old Livery Barn, Mason City

house with three small rooms. The school teacher stayed there, because my mother went to Lincoln, for appendicitis -- I always had to button the teacher's shoes. I just had one teacher from chart class to 8th grade. In the 9th grade I had a new teacher.

I rode a burrow my Grandfather Peterson had given me. I had it for two or three years. Grandfather Peterson kept him on his farm most of the time.

I saw my first car when I was eight, but not

many people had cars until years later.[1] I drove my first car in 1914. My Uncle Charlie Lamb was married to my mother's youngest sister. He ran the garage. He sold Model T's and Reos. When someone bought a car, the dealer had to teach them to drive. The veterinarian in Mason City rented a Model T Ford from Uncle Charlie, but was scared to death of cars. He asked if I could drive a car, and I said yes, but I had never really driven a car. I had driven around the block before then, but that was all. I drove him out into the country to deliver a calf. He never let anyone else drive him after that. Of course, the car didn't have any fenders. A little rain and all the mud and stuff would fly all over you.

My dad bought two tires for his Ford Touring car, at $26 a piece that were guaranteed 3,000 miles. If they'd go flat, you could drive home with them on, because the tires didn't have any cords. You couldn't go too far without getting a flat tire in those days. Towns would have nails all over the place. Nails were square. Mason City had a long magnetic rod drug by a horse that picked up nails, but most anything would puncture a tire with no cords.

We got milk from a farmer who delivered it in a horse and buggy. Milk cost 5 cents a gallon. Sometimes, if the farmer had one left over, he'd just give it to us. A loaf of bread was 10 cents. We never had any crackers. Eggs were 8 or 10 cents a dozen. Up to the time the state of Nebraska went dry, the saloons sold a

Chapter 2 - 1910-1919

sandwich and a beer for 5 cents. You could get a gallon of beer for a nickel. Sandwiches were on the counter 24 hours a day. The saloons never closed, but because they gave so much food away, most of them went broke and were forced to shut down.

Wymer's Hardware, Mason City, Nebraska. Harve Keller, front right behind counter

My dad had a lot of different jobs. He worked the dray wagon until around when Twila was born, around 1911 or 12. Then he became Town Marshall. He was Town Marshall for eight years. Before World War I, he worked in Wymer's Hardware store. Right after the war, he ran a restaurant. Ma cooked in the restaurant and people would come from all around to eat her meals. About 1920, he bought the hotel. They did that until 1923 when they moved to Grand Island.

In 1914 and 1915, I worked for another farmer,

Luther Rummery. It was about a mile and a quarter out of town and I could walk up town on weekends. I had a saddle horse and he let me keep it out there and, in the evening, I would run up town.

Once, I got 22 stings from a nest of bumble bees when I worked on the farm in the fall of 1914. In the spring of 1915, a chicken got away and as I was chasing it, my foot went down in a thawed out pile of manure, and I ran my foot through a pitch fork that was in the pile. I went to the doctor. The doctor, Dr. Rummery, Luther's brother, heated the rod that was stored perpendicular to the side of the stove out of the way. Once the rod was pulled, the rod was horizontal and could be used to hang wet clothing on, and the heat from the stove would dry the clothes. It was straight on the end. The doctor told my Dad to hold me. I could smell the burning flesh. Good thing Dad was strong, or I would've killed him -- but that's the way things were done in those days.

As one of my jobs as a teen, I worked for my sister Lorena's husband, Wayne Coxen, on Saturdays. I'd haul dirt and take dirt to roads and smooth it out. Everybody liked Wayne. He served in World War I. About a year after he came home from the war, he died of anemia. He was buried in Mason City. They had a six gun salute, and I shot one of those guns.

When I was 15, I was more like a ten year old as far as knowing who I was. I hadn't really found myself as a young teen. Some kids played tricks. There was a smokehouse to smoke meat behind the market. A kid said to me, "Hey come here." He locked me in, but he came back and said, "You've been in there long enough." Then he let me out. I wasn't scared. I never got into trouble, tore things up or gambled.

There were some tough kids in Mason City during my teens. A trick they did on Halloween night was to get a whole yard of machinery and take it all apart and put it on top of the opera house. The opera house was two stories and had a gabled roof. They pulled the machinery up by pieces, plows, rakes, wheels they had taken off something, and pulled it up by a rope. They'd put the wheels back on, so they'd have to be taken apart to take them down.

In 1915, when I was in the 10th grade, when school started up, the school closed for six weeks because of an outbreak of smallpox. When it reopened, I went back to school for two days and they said I had verloid,[2] it was some kind of a reaction to the shot they gave me for smallpox. School didn't seem worth it. I went home. I told my Mother, and she said, "There's the washing machine handle." Late that fall, I went to work on the railroad for a while as a section hand.

In April, 1916, a couple of friends of mine, Delbert Wilson and Albert Davis, and I bummed our way out west on a freight train out of Mason City. The bumming trip was in the days when bums road the trains. We reached Seneca, Nebraska, 250 miles west of Mason City, where the crew always stopped to eat dinner. The engineer and the cops came to the box car and told us they were taking us to jail. There was a woman, Mrs. Hoyt, who ran the restaurant, who said, "Hello, Warren. What are you doing here?"

"Guess I'm going to jail," I told her.

"I know him. We grew up neighbors," she told the engineer and the cops. So they let us back on the train. I was lucky that I ran into someone I knew that fed the railroad crew. They said that when we got back on the train, to stay out of sight. When we got up to Alliance, Nebraska, we got off the freight and got on a passenger train. We rode in the coal car of the passenger train. We rode this train for 12 to 15 miles. Then the engineer stopped the train and came back to us with a pistol in his hand and said, "Come down off of there, boys." So, we got off in the wide open spaces in Wyoming. It was just about nightfall. A fellow came along and told us that the freight train stopped at a corral, if a loaded stock car was there. If there wasn't any stock car to pick up, they didn't stop, but they slowed down to check. When the train slowed down, that's when we got on. The next day, we got off at Sheridan, Wyoming. Even though it was April, it was cold and there was snow on the ground.

Delbert Wilson went to the barber shop where he was told that King's Ranch needed three workers. I worked at King's Ranch for about five to six weeks. Albert Davis worked there for less than a week when he got a wire that his brother had drowned. So he went

Chapter 2 - 1910-1919

back home.

    I worked with a stone-bolt, a kind of a sled, and I put it on the end of a wagon. I'd find an old cow that had a calf. The cow would be too weak because she had been out on the range and had not much to eat. We'd pull the calf up. We'd stay close to the wagon, because the cow may chase you. We'd take them back and feed them. I worked for periods of three days driving a chuck wagon with four horses for cowboys who took cows up to Cloud Peak, which was 10,000 feet high, when I was at King's Ranch.

    When I got done at King's Ranch, I went to a dude ranch and got a job there. The Eaton Brother's Dude Ranch was the first one in the United States. It

Warren and Men from the Bridge Gang.
Left to right: Leonard Lamb, Another Cousin, Allen Oakley, and Warren, 1917-1918

was located in the Bighorn Mountain range, 12 miles out of Sheridan, Wyoming. I stayed there until August and saddled horses. People from the East came for a vacation. I decided that I didn't want any more of that bumming. It wasn't for me. So I went back home.

The next Spring, in 1917, I went to work for a bridge building company, Allied Contractors, that was building a bridge near Mason City. Allied Contractors's headquarters were located outside of Omaha, Nebraska. The company built bridges all over Nebraska, in the Black Hills of South Dakota, and in Wyoming. I worked with the bridge gang for six or seven years. At first, I only earned 25 cents an hour, later it went to 60 cents.

After working around Mason City for about three weeks, the gang moved on to Ansley, Nebraska to work on the bridge over the dam. Then we went to Sargent

Draft Registration Card, 1918

and then Gates, then Oconto, which was south of

Broken Bow. There were a bunch of little bridges that we contracted for over a lot of little creeks. In 1918, we came to Grand Island for about four or five months to build bridges between St. Paul and Grand Island. When I was there, I bought an Overland car. The axle broke. Axles broke easily in those days.

I did not serve in the military during World War I. I turned 18 in January of the year that World War I ended. But, of course, I registered.

ENDNOTES

1. *Mason City 1886-1976,* A Bicentennial Project, Callaway, NE: Loup Valley Queen, 1976, 3.

2. Note: Authors' spelling is as it sounds when pronounced.

Chapter 3
1920-1929

The Roaring 20s

The early part of the '20s, I worked on the bridge gang. In 1921-22, the bridge gang went to the Black Hills. We worked out of the little town of Hermosa, in the Black Hills, South Dakota, two years. Hermosa was between Rapid City and Hot Springs. When we were there, we had a dynamiting crew. The crew used horses to level the roads after the dynamiting. I didn't dynamite, because I'd get bad headaches from being around it. We'd dig coffer dams, put the pilings in, and build a frame at the top. They made us mix the cement for 10 minutes -- ordinarily we'd mix it just three or four minutes. There were no roads in the Black Hills, just trails. We were building bridges at the same time that the road crews were building roads.

The Green River Bridge in Wyoming that we built in 1923 was the biggest bridge we built. It was about five miles west of Green River on Highway 30. In Green River, we always had three crews -- one coming, one there, one going. The turnover was high. Freight trains would come by and guys would work for two or three days for their meals and then leave. A lot of my work was going to town, running errands, and helping pack steel beams. I'd get a half of beef every day to feed the gang. It'd take a couple days for the crew to eat a whole cow. Sometimes the bosses would ask me to go get whiskey for them. They would give me $60 for a gallon of moonshine and I would get one for $45 and keep the change. I ran all of their errands. At Green River, a whole dinner at a restaurant was 25 cents including dessert. Coffee went with the meal, otherwise, it was 5 cents.

It was just like the Old West when I worked in Green River. In town, there were beer parlors. Guys'd get drunk and shoot holes in the roof. Anyone could have a gun until the U.S. went dry in 1918. In Green River, men still packed guns, but they kinda stopped it when they went into the cities or they'd just have their guns taken away. The first room of a beer parlor was where men played pool. The second room was for gambling. Men had to leave their guns before going into the gambling room. Then the last room was where the ladies were that gave the guys a good time. There was one street that was so rough that even the cops wouldn't go on it. If you went on that street, you would go there at your own risk.

In the early fall of 1923, after we had gotten the Green River bridge built, two friends and I bought an old Model T Ford Touring car for about $60. We wanted to drive it from Wyoming to Nebraska. We started east and took U. S. Highway 30 all the way. In many places in Wyoming, Highway 30 was not much more than a wagon trail. We came down from Green River and passed through Medicine Bow. One of my friends was driving. We were coming down a grade and

Chapter 3 - 1920-1929

the road turned. He couldn't handle the curve and he upset the car. The three of us got the car upright, cars were not that heavy in those days. I drove from then on, but the car was so badly out of align that we nearly didn't make it. We found a house between Medicine Bow and Rawlins where a guy had some tools and I got the car back into alignment. At times, on the way between Rawlins and Laramie, the road would disappear into the sagebrush and, at times, we had to follow the railroad tracks by driving in the ditch along the tracks to get where we wanted to go.

When we got to Laramie, a farmer flagged us down on the road and waved his arms to get us to stop. He asked us if we would head the lettuce for him. He said he would pay the three of us a total of $10 a day. We worked ten hours a day. We slept in the barn and ate meals on the back porch. We did that for four days. The farmer, he was a Swede and a nice man, wanted us to dig his potatoes, but we decided we didn't want to stay any longer.

When we got to Cheyenne, we had to overhaul the car's engine. I was afraid that the rods would go out in it before we got home. After I tightened the rods, the car worked fine. When we left Cheyenne, we drove straight through to Grand Island. It took us 24 hours of driving round the clock to travel the 325 miles.

When we got to Grand Island, one of my friends was picked up by the FBI. I don't know what he did. The other friend decided to go back east and so I was left with the car.

I worked on the bridge gang until December of 1924. My folks had moved to Grand Island the year before. I didn't even know that they had moved until I got a letter from my Mom that came from Grand Island. I thought they were still in Mason City. When the folks moved to Grand Island in 1923, they lived first at 208 North Bogg St. They moved from there to 8th and Elm and then to 517 W. 8th. My sister Lorena and her three kids lived with the folks after her husband, Wayne, died right after WW I. In 1925, she bought the house at 1204 West Ninth Street that they all they lived in for many years.

Grand Island was founded in 1857 by a few farm produce settlers who sold to travelers. The town was moved 5 miles to the north of the first settlement in 1866 to be by the Union Pacific Railroad. It grew from a trading post and mule-buying center to be a distribution and manufacturing hub. When I moved to town, Third Street was the busiest street in the city. If you cut across the dummy

Third Street, Grand Island, Early 1920s. Courtesy of Stuhr Museum

Chapter 3 - 1920-1929

in the middle of the intersection, you got pinched. You had to drive clear around it.

The old Union Pacific Depot located on Front and Locust Streets was just east of where to station is today. President Harding's funeral train went through here. I waited for it and watched the train go by.

When I came to Grand

Union Pacific Railroad Station, Grand Island, Early 1920s. Courtesy of Stuhr Museum

Marie W. Kuehner, on the Kuehner Homestead, Doniphan, 1926

Island in December of '24, I decided that I had had enough of working on the bridge gang. My Dad was working for the City of Grand Island, but not long after I got home, he got sick. I worked in his place two to five weeks. Then, on May 5, 1925, at noon, I went to work for the City full time.

I never did know why they were called the roaring 20s. Everything was going good, there were no wars, -- people were going to the dances, nothing affected your normal living. Guys were interested in getting cars. They'd get a sticker from every place they went through and put it on their car to prove they had been there. Driving 100 miles was like going to China now.

There was no big boom, but nothing was holding anybody back. Everybody was kind of happy. Girls wore what we called hobble skirts, and girls were referred to as Flappers and Guineas.

I bought my first new car, a Model T Roadster, for $425 in early 1926. Not long after that, I began dating Marie Kuehner of Doniphan, Nebraska. I met her on a double date. Later, she told me that the other gal was supposed to be my date.

We were married on December 24, 1926 in the Hall County Court House, Grand Island. On the night before I was married, I stayed at the Kuehner farm because the weather was bad. It was so foggy on the day we got married that we could hardly see to get to town. When the official started marrying us, he wanted to

Warren and Marie on a date, in his new Model T Roadster, 1926

Chapter 3 - 1920-1929

know if I had any proof that Marie was 21 years of age. Marie was born on December 24, 1905, she was one day shy of her 21st birthday. I told him to ask her. Just then, Marie's mother, Rosa, stuck her head in the door and said, "Marie is of age."

We didn't have a special honeymoon, but we went a few places later on that were like honeymoons. Marie's brother Bill gave a party for us and a lot of people came. Not all the people could get into the house.

Marie and Warren's wedding picture, 1926

Our first home was at 1103 West 8th Street in Grand Island. We rented from an old fella by the name of Davis. Davis said, "I'm going to California for six months. I'd like to have you take care of the house 'til I get back." So I did, but when we went into the house, there were dishes on the table and every thing was cluttered. When the six months were over, we moved into a garage bungalow on the alley at 1515 North Cedar. We were there about two or three months.

Marie was a good cook. She cooked like my mother did. Everything tasted good and was cooked just right. I really liked her homemade bread. At first, she had a time of it cooking for just two. She had always cooked for large groups, like when the threshers came.

Marie just kind of took life as it came under the circumstances. We did a lot of socializing and we took trips in the Model T. We probably put 500 miles on the car each month, although you couldn't tell for sure with cars in those days. We'd go out in the country and drop in on people. Everybody did it. You didn't have to make an appointment to see people. You just went. If they were doing chores, you'd pitch in and help and then maybe stay for supper. When the farm people came to town, they would do the same thing. They would just drop in.

We'd go to Omaha and it would take 7 1/2 hours one way. Going to Lincoln would take about four. You couldn't go more than 25 miles an hour because the roads were so washboardy. But Marie and I both liked to travel and did a lot of it.

We liked to dance and would go out on Saturday night to local ballrooms. We also would play cards with friends. We did a lot of things with Heine and Ruby Schoel. Heine worked as a engineer in the ice house with the City.

Being married to Marie turned out to be a wonderful deal.

I was never very much of a politician. If a presidential election would come along, I voted for the party and if the city election came along I voted for whoever I wanted. Teddy Roosevelt is the first President I remember, but I never voted for anyone but a

Chapter 3 - 1920-1929

Democrat in presidential elections. I started to vote in 1921 and the first presidential election I voted in was in 1924.

In 1925, Ted Elsberry, who was from Chicago, and I were just sitting and talking and he asked if I had registered to vote in Grand Island. I said, "No," and he said, "Let's get it done." So we went upstairs in city hall and registered. We voted in the city elections and I voted Democrat that time, but I generally voted for whoever I thought would do the best job..

When I first went to work for the City in 1925, it was with the Water Department. At the time, Ted Elsberry worked for the Union Pacific as a yard foreman. He told the railroad folks that he was going to run for mayor of Grand Island. They told him that, if he ran for mayor, he would be fired. He ran and got fired. He got elected. Elsberry served one term as mayor and then Clarence Burdick, the boss at the City Electric and Water, hired him as a Water foreman. Burdick gave Elsberry a raise, because he had been at the top.

Elsberry took me along on the job, because he didn't know the job well and so I helped him do his job right. He'd ask me and I'd tell him what to do. So, I told Burdick, "If I'm going to run this job, give me five cents an hour more." Burdick said, "Give him a dime."

For seven years I did a little of everything they had. I worked a couple of years putting water service to houses. I didn't much like the work. We were building an eight inch water main around the edge of town and six inch mains so there was circulation to all those water pipes to the houses. One winter I helped an electrician with a generator. It takes a couple days to shut one down and start it up. One winter they got short handed, and I pulled ice cakes out of the ice house. I did everything until 1932. That's when I started reading electric meters because I wanted a steady job.

In 1928, I bought my first radio, a 10-tube Mohawk Lyric. I had heard a radio for the first time in 1923. At night, I'd try to get stations from all over the country, but it was difficult sometimes because the stations faded out. Every Saturday night, I'd listen to the Grand Ol' Opry out of Nashville on WSM. I listened to KFAQ in St. Joseph, Missouri. It had good old time country music, but like many of the stations, it was on only a couple of hours a day. KMMJ, in Clay Center, Nebraska, was the only station around Grand Island. On Saturday night, WEAF from New York City had good news and classical music. Other stations I listened to were KOA in Denver, WWL in New Orleans, WGN and WMAQ in Chicago and KFI in Los Angeles. On Sundays, the stations could broadcast church services, but, for the longest time, there was mostly silence otherwise on Sundays. I sure enjoyed listening to that radio.

Chapter 4
1930-1939

A Time of Birth and Building

In early 1930, Marie and I found out that we were going to have a baby. Our son Bill was born on August 15, 1930. We named him William Henry, but we always called him Bill. From the start, he was a sickly child. At the time, we were living in a house at 618 W. 11th Street that was owned by my mother-in-law, Rosa Kuehner. When Bill was born, she decided to come to town and live with us. She lived with us until 1934.

1932 was both a good and bad year for us. Grand Island celebrated the 75th Anniversary of its founding. All the men were told to grow beards so I grew one.

In 1932, I got the steady job of reading electric meters. I read the meters in the city and the other guy read the meters in the country and little towns.

But the Great Depression was also beginning to

Warren, Grand Island's 75th Year Celebration, 1932

have its way. I had a job all through it, but the City cut us all to pieces in the Spring 1932. I was getting $129 a month and was cut to $85 a month. They cut everyone else too. The City worked nine hours a day, so that gave me $3.15 a day, and I worked six days a week. I only made 35 cents an hour after they cut me. I had no vacation, no insurance, no pension plans, no sick leave. Everything that came along was at your expense.

At least I had a job. All my friends were out of work or went to work for the WPA (Works Progress Administration, part of the New Deal).

In 1932, I bought a Chevy Coupe. It had a place built in the front fenders for the wire wheeled spare tires. It was a sport coupe. I paid $680 for it. I sure

Warren's 1932 Chevy Coupe

liked that car. We went all over in it. By that time, the roads were getting better. We could go 30 to 35 miles an hour. We could make it to Lincoln in 3 hours. We made lots of trips. Sometimes on the spur of the moment. I'd come home on a Friday night and say, "Let's go to the Black Hills" and Marie would say, "Let's go." Marie was good about going along with whatever I wanted to do. So, we'd throw the suitcase into the car and go to the Black Hills. It was 425 miles to Hot Springs, S. D. We liked to go where we didn't know people.

We would visit the radio stations. We'd go to Clay Center, which was right outside of Kearney, and go to KMMJ. We'd watch them broadcast their programs. We went in the '32 Chevy with Heine and Ruby Schoel to KMA in Shenandoah, Iowa. The people at the stations were real friendly and asked us what music we wanted them to play.

Over the years, we went to a lot of dances at the Glovera Ballroom on 4th and Cedar. Big name bands and well-known bands from the area would play there. The big name bands would stop and play there when they were touring from the East Coast to the West Coast.

Lawrence Welk and his band came to town in 1934. He played at the Glovera. He had 8 to 10 musicians in his band. He was living in North Dakota then. He only came to Grand Island a couple of times, but we sure liked his music.

Saturday nights was always a big social night in Grand Island. It had been that way for years. Everyone in town, it seemed like, would go downtown. I don't know when people first started doing this, but they were doing it when I first moved to Grand Island. Marie and I did it when we were first married. In some of the earlier years that we did it, some people were still coming to town with horses. People would be in the streets.

When cars were more plentiful, generally, a couple of neighbors or friends would drive their cars downtown in the afternoon and park one in front of Kaufman's store. Then they would go back home with their neighbor or friend. Then at night, they would go back down to Kaufman's with their neighbor or friend, and park the second car wherever they could, sometimes it might be six or eight blocks away because it was so crowded. Then they would sit in the car they had brought in the afternoon and watch the people, visit, and make new acquaintances.

It wasn't until 8:00 p.m. or after by the time the farmers got uptown. Most of the activity took place around 10 or 11 at night. The stores stayed open as long as there was business. Grocery stores stayed open until 12 or 12:30 in the morning. It was just a way of life.

My father-in-law, Richard Kuehner, died of cancer on May 31, 1933 at the age of 68. The next year, in 1934, my mother-in-law was still staying with us in the house at 618 W. 11th Street and she came home one day and said that she had sold the house. She didn't give us a chance to buy it or anything and so we had to move. We moved to 232 South Sycamore.

Chapter 4 - 1930-1939

Warren, baby Rosemarie, and 6 year old Bill, in the Park, 2300 block, West 3rd, Grand Island, 1936

In late 1935, we learned that we were going to have another child. On June 11, 1936, Rosemarie was born in the house on Sycamore Street.

In 1936, Marie's mother, Rosa Bosselman Kuehner, wanted Billy baptized, so, I joined St. Pauls Lutheran Church and got baptized with Bill.

In 1934, the weather began to change. The drought started and lasted until 1937. There was hardly any moisture in the air. The drought spread all over the mid-west and south. We began to have terrible dust storms. The winters became colder. The weather in 1936 was the worst.

In the summer, there were dust storms. When I was in the country reading meters, I'd have to turn around and wait for the dust to go down, because I couldn't see across the intersection. I couldn't leave the windows up because there was no air conditioning. I looked like I had been in a coal bin. And it was hot.

We had no fans, no air conditioners to help us with the heat. When the hot wind and dust blew, I'd wet towels and put them in the windows to keep the dust out and get a little fresh air. At night there, I'd wet down the big porch on the house on Sycamore Street and get a little air without so much dirt.

In the last two weeks of February 1936, the temperature never got above zero, day or night. I sure got cold. As I read meters, everybody had a quilt over their back door to keep the cold out, so I'd have to go around to the front. I'd have to go where the snow was scooped out. It was so deep, you couldn't wade through it.

Marie, baby Rosemarie, and 6 year old Bill, in the Park, 2300 block, West 3rd, Grand Island, 1936

I had to get Bill from school because he had bad circulation and couldn't tell when he was cold. Usually I'd get done reading meters around 1:30 in the afternoon but, in cold weather, it would be 6:30 in the evening, because I had to stop to take Bill to school and

Chapter 4 - 1930-1939

then go get him. There was no heater in the car either.

Over the years, I had fixed up the house on Sycamore to suit me. Then in the summer of 1936, the landlord told me he was going to raise the rent from $20 to $25 a month. I was only making $85 a month and so I couldn't afford to live there anymore. We had to move again.

We moved first to the upstairs of the big house at 118 West 9th. After we moved again to 2403 West 4th, I was prompted to build a house. I was tired of moving and decided to get a house of my own no matter what. That's when I arranged to build the house at 412 West 16th.

I wanted a little bigger house than I was able to build but, in those days, you had to have two-thirds down. The house cost $2,200 to build and I borrowed the difference as a straight loan at 5% interest. I only had to pay the interest each month. The principal was due at the end of the loan period. The loan I had was for five years.

My house was the last one in Grand Island to have its foundation dug out by a team of horses. We moved in on May 5, 1937. What I remember most about moving in was that I had a kid that raised heck. Rosemarie just didn't like it there at first. It didn't seem like home for her.

When we first moved into it, the house was bare. There were not many plugs in the basement. There was one light at the bottom of the stairs on a string. We had no light fixtures. There was a sidewalk in the front. We had electric and water, but the gas was not hooked up until the next day.

    I began to work to improve the house and was able to do most of the work myself. I put a stool in in the basement. I dug it out, put in the plumbing, and

412 West 16th Street, Grand Island, 1937

then ran the pipes to connect the washing machine.

    About the time we moved to West 16th street, I gave Marie the job of handling the finances. She was good at it. Every penny would go where she wanted it to. She used to walk up town and go to all the grocery stores and save all the pennies she could. She did everything to help me all she could. She watched every little bargain she could get. We had no icebox, deep freeze (there were none those days), so we couldn't stock anything, only what we could can. We bought

Chapter 4 - 1930-1939

peaches by the bushel and canned them. That was our Labor Day job. I always helped her.

Every one of the working people was in the same boat. Their kids didn't know any different. Penney's used to have a white sale every year. They had pretty good sales. We probably wouldn't have had so much if I would have had to do the money end of it. Marie was good at it. To me, the times weren't really hard, I just took it in stride.

I went to work at the Eagles, the Fraternal Order of Eagles, on Saturdays and Sundays to get the loan on the house paid off. I worked at the Eagles all my spare time to pay on it. I ran the bar and took care of the slot machines. Marie did her part. She waited tables at the Eagles while I was running the bar. It was the happiest time of our married life

I could get along with people, so, in 1939, I was asked me to take over collecting unpaid electric bills. I took over all electric meter business, did everything but the hiring and firing. If they didn't get their work done, it was up to the City to get after them. I'd put the guys on a route. I picked the work I wanted. That's the way it landed. I turned the residences over to the other fellas.

I wanted to do my job right, but I didn't like it when Burdick said to me, "Don't offend anyone," as I was set to begin the country route. I handed him the route cards I had in my hand and said, "Don't tell me how to do my job. After I get back from reading meters, then we can talk." He never said anything like that to me again.

When I began to read meters and collect bills in the rural areas, one place I collected in was St. Libory, a small farming community north of Grand Island. I always knew when to let the farmers not pay their bills. They could only pay when had something to sell, either their crops or their livestock. They always paid and I knew they would. The city never lost any money because I gave farmers extra time to pay.

Once a month, I read meters and collected in St. Libory, Worms and the surrounding country. I'd go into St. Libory after I had read the meters and sit down in the beer parlor. I'd sit there and make out bills. I knew the guys would all come in for a beer. And that's when I got the money for their electric bills.

Chapter 5
1940-1949

War and Expanding Horizons

In 1940, the nation was pretty much out of the Depression. Most people who wanted them had jobs. I found that fewer people had delinquent electric bills as I collected for the city. But I was beginning to worry because Hitler had started the war in Europe.

December 7, 1941 was Pearl Harbor. The neighbor boy who lived on the corner of 16th and Cedar, Don Gockley, came running across the street, yelling, "They bombed Pearl Harbor." The next morning, Rosemarie was taking off her overshoes in the hall outside of the first grade classroom at West Lawn Elementary School and said to Nona Falmlen, "Japan bombed Pearl Harbor." "I know," Nona said, as she pulled off her own overshoes. Rosemarie felt fear hanging in the air at the school that morning "That hallway scene was very vivid in my mind for a long time."

Grand Island became involved in the war effort. It had an army air base located here. The city had so many servicemen that, on Saturday nights, Third Street was thick with men in brown uniforms. At each intersection stood military police wearing black armbands with the letters, "MP," on them.

As the war went on, B-17s and fighter planes would train all day. Later, B-29s came to the air base to train. Those big planes really made a racket when they flew low. Sometimes they didn't miss the tree tops by more than 25 feet as they were taking off. When they got around to putting a super charger on them, then they flew more like 150 feet above the tree tops. When they flew so low to the ground, you could see them as if they were on the ground. You could feel the wind after they passed. Cats and dogs would hardly go outside when the big planes were flying. They would fly around four to five hours at a time. Sometimes, when they flew in formation, Mustangs would dive down in between them, practicing.

During the war, we had more soldiers here than residents. The city was packed. People couldn't find places to live. The city built 16 houses in one block on South Locust. And they built other houses. I finished my basement and rented it out to a soldier and his wife.

Not long after the war started, rationing began. You just got so much food. We saved tokens to purchase scarce commodities and stretched the dollar to meet the needs of the family. You could only get two or three cans of beans a month. Marie would put red and blue tokens in a small crystal glass in the cupboard, when the time came to buy food, she would reach for the glass. Everything was hard to get. Meat was very hard to get, so we got it only once a week. You might have a ration chip, but the stores would be out when you'd go after it.

Chapter 5 - 1940-1949

Gasoline was rationed, so people had to share rides to get where they needed to go. I couldn't get tires for my car, so I sold it. I got a pretty good price for it, but it meant that we didn't have a car of our own until well after the war. During the war, the only car I drove was the one the City owned, the one I drove for work.

1941 Ford, Warren Drove on His Job

Marie and I worked extra jobs to meet expenses. I was still working at the Eagles, running the bar on Saturdays and Sundays. Marie kept working at the Eagles waiting tables for a while after the war started, but then she went to work at the Quaker Oat defense plant that made bombs.

When the time was up on the loan that we had on the house, we still had a little left to pay. So we took out another loan, this one was for one year. By 1943, we had it all paid off. We paid for the house in six years. It took us working all the extra that we could to do it. But we did it, and it was worth it.

One day, Marie was working at the defense plant and was working at the end of a long assembly line right before the bombs left the plant. A cart carrying a 500 pound bomb tipped and fell on her leg. The bomb had no igniting fuse, so it couldn't explode, but it broke her leg.

Rosemarie tells me that on the day her mother got hurt. "I did not see my mother that day. My father took us over to stay at my Grandma Keller's. Later, my mother showed me the dent in her thigh the handle of the bomb cart had made." The dent never righted itself her entire life.

"We practiced blackouts, both at home and at school," Rosemarie says, "At home, we'd snuggle at the base of the large floor style General Electric 10-tube radio. And there was also a curfew of 10:30 p.m." Those blackouts were for Civil Defense No one was allowed to even light a cigarette. It had to be totally black.

In 1944, my Dad retired from working with the City. He and my mother planned to move to Hillsboro, Oregon, which is 17 miles west of Portland. They planned to go out there around Christmas 1944.

My mother went out to Oregon ahead of him on a train, but Dad wanted to take his car out there and needed someone to drive it for him. I was going to drive him out there if Marie would go with us. She was working at the defense plant and I wanted her to quit and go with us, but she wasn't sure she wanted to go. We had Merle "Ping" Fairfield, he was from Mason City, lined up to drive Dad out there if Marie and I didn't go. Marie quit her job a couple of days before Dad was to leave for Oregon, so we went. Merle also decided to go along. My sister Lorena stayed in Grand Island with our

Chapter 5 - 1940-1949

two kids.

Rationing was still on and so we had to make arrangements to get enough coupons to be able to buy enough gas to get out to Oregon. It was Christmas day, 1944 when we left. It was 1600 miles to Hillsboro. We took Highway 30 all the way. It wasn't paved in many places, but it was pretty good road.

We took the better share of five days to get there because my father wouldn't let me drive over 45 mph. When we stopped to fill up the gas tank the first time, I check the oil and found out that it was barely on the stick. The car wasn't burning oil, it was leaking it. I knew that it was going to take quite a bit of oil to get us to the Coast. The car worked good, it was just losing oil. I asked Dad what he wanted to do. He asked me how much oil it would take to get to Oregon. I said about a case, twenty-four quarts. He said, "Okay, let's buy the oil and keep going."

We stayed at Cheyenne the first night. On the second day, I stepped on the brakes and there weren't any. I stopped in the next town, which was not far, and bought some brake fluid. I was fortunate that I didn't have to drain the brake lines to get air bubbles out. I had to fill the brake fluid three times on the way out.

The second night we stayed in Cameron, Wyoming and the third night we stayed in Twin Falls, Idaho. The fourth night we stayed in La Grande, Oregon in the foothills of the Blue Mountains. The straight wind blew so hard that we could hardly stand up.

On the fifth day, it was raining as we were going up the mountain, but, as we went further up, it turned to snow. On the other side, it kept snowing until we got far enough down then it turned to rain again.

When we got about 60 miles from Hillsboro, we were coming down a steep cliff about a 1000 feet above the Columbia River. The road down the cliff had three turn back curves on the way down. We were near the top and going down the hill, when the brakes went out. I stepped on them and there was nothing. On that road there were no turn outs, so I put the car in second gear and the engine held it back as we went down. At the bottom of the cliff, there was the small town of The Dalles.

For some reason, it was Christmas in Oregon. Oregon had a different day to celebrate Christmas then than the rest of us did. In the small town, everybody must have been celebrating, because I couldn't find anybody to get me some brake fluid.

I went into a beer parlor. The place was crowded with people who had drunk too much. I asked the woman at the bar if there was anybody who could get me some brake fluid. The woman said that there was no mechanic in there. She pointed me to a guy who was sitting across the room and I asked the guy if he knew where I could find a mechanic. He pointed to a guy who was sleeping and said that he was a mechanic. So we woke the guy up and told him what I needed. He said he was willing to go to his garage and get me some

Chapter 5 - 1940-1949

fluid. We had to hold him up to get him across the street to his garage. The mechanic put some brake fluid in a pop bottle and I poured it into the brake cylinder. It took about half of it. I pumped the brakes once or twice and they held, so we took off. We had no more car trouble after that, but we did use about twenty quarts of oil on the trip.

We got to Hillsboro in the real early evening. We stopped and ate supper before we went to the house. My mother was upset at my dad when we got to the house because she had held up dinner for us. She had told my father before he left Grand Island that she would hold dinner until we got there. He had just forgotten that she had told him.

Marie and I stayed four or five days and went all over the country around Oregon and into Washington. I had to get back to work, so we came back on the Union Pacific. The train had a big steam engine. It took us twenty eight hours to come back. The train was scheduled to lay over for five hours in Cheyenne. When we got to Cheyenne, we were six hours behind schedule. They cut three hours off the layover time and made up the other three hours between Cheyenne and Grand Island. The engineer had the train going about 95 miles an hour at times. We got to Grand Island on time. It was a trip I will always treasure.

After the war, I continued to work for the city. I enjoyed my work because I was always good at working with people and getting them to pay their overdue electric bills.

Rosemarie says, "During my own growing up period, Dad had a real desire to take care of his family. He took my Grandmother Rosa Bosselman Kuehner into his home when she needed a place to live. One time Grandma Kuehner fell ill and my mother also was sick. He took care of both of them and got my brother and me up in the morning, fed, and off to school, and then went out and did a day's work at his own job. He even braided my hair."

In 1946, I took the family to see my parents in Hillsboro . We went out on the Union Pacific's Streamliner. When we got there, we borrowed my dad's car and went sightseeing. The sights were beautiful. We saw the beautiful winding mountain Highway 101 (near the coast and runs through Washington, Oregon and California). We saw waterfalls in Oregon off Highway 30 in the Columbia Gorge National Scenic Area.[1] Some of them were Multnomah Falls, Horsetail Falls, and Wahkeena Falls, and Sahalie Falls which is near Mt. Hood and the Hood River. We circled around Mt. Hood on a WPA (Works Progress Administration) road that Roosevelt built during the war. We had a picnic about half way around. We also saw the Columbia River by the Bonneville Dam and a Fish Ladder at the Dam. Trout could swim back up the River to spawn. And, of course, we saw the Pacific Ocean."

In 1946, our friend, Ava Haymann, came back to Grand Island and took my family in her Buick to her

Chapter 5 - 1940-1949   57

home in Colorado Springs. The Haymanns had lived in Grand Island and had moved to Colorado about six months before. Her husband, Arthur, had been in the jewelry business in Grand Island. When were in Colorado, we saw the Garden of the Gods and the Will Rogers' Station. We sat in the Haymann's backyard and watched the fireworks from Pikes Peak. At the end of the visit, Ava brought us back to Grand Island.

In 1946, Bill dropped out of Grand Island Senior High School to work odd jobs and at the gas company He did odd jobs at carnivals that were in town, collected for the *Independent*, sold on the street corner for both the *Independent* and *World-Herald*, and worked for the Western Union before he got on regular jobs. Bill had trouble holding jobs because his health was never good.

My sister Etna had three daughters, Lucille, Wanda and Virginia. The three girls decided to get

Sloggett Daughters, Triple Wedding,
June 30, 1946

married at the same time. On June 30, 1946, they had a triple wedding in the Christian Church. I gave away Lucille. She married Elmer Goehring. Juan Sloggett, the sisters' father, gave away Wanda. She married Ray Feierfeil and Wesley Sloggett gave away Virginia. She married Jim Sanders.

Rosemarie wanted a dog and so we got Butch in 1947. I never did like that dang dog. Marie would have him on a rope leash. He would chew the rope in two, and, when he was certain Marie wasn't looking, he would run away. Dogs belong on a farm where they can run free in the wide open spaces.

Butch, 1947

I always liked to help my kids with their work when I could. In the 1947-48 school year, Rosemarie was required to take a sewing class. Marie had always wanted Rosemarie to learn to sew because she did not know how herself. Rosemarie says, "I was having difficulty making a yellow, Swiss, polka dot blouse. My father got down on the living room floor with me and my pattern and helped me cut the pieces for the blouse. Then he read the directions with me and we figured out how to put it together, or we

Chapter 5 - 1940-1949

thought we had, because I sewed the sleeve of the blouse in backward. We laughed. We knew it didn't look right.

"My father and mother were very involved in my activities. First as a Brownie Scout, then as an Intermediate Girl Scout. In particular, I remember my father faithfully eating a Kellogg's Krumble Bran cereal so that I could complete my collection for a badge of all the pictures of birds. Another time, he and my mother helped me collect and mount leaves for a badge. We collected some of the leaves at my Grandparent Kellers' home in Oregon. Dad made a beautiful wooden cover to this book. A brown shoe string holds the pages of leaves between the cover. My father put a coat of varnish on the covers down the basement in what we called, 'the furnace room.' One other time, we were collecting drift wood for a girl scout project. My father helped me sand it, varnish it, and then he wired it for a small light.

Rosemarie and Bill, 1947

"My father spent a lot of time with my brother, Bill, whose interest was in genealogy" Yes, Bill and I spent a lot of time together going to cemeteries to trace family history.

In 1948, we had bad blizzards. I had to go out and put up the power lines that the blizzards knocked down.

My sister, Etna, was sick at the time. During one of the blizzards, I went to Omaha to get her and bring her back to Grand Island. It snowed all the way down. When Etna's son-in-law, Ray Feierfeil, her daughter Wanda and I were coming back with her, the weather got very bad. Ray drove with a spotlight on the side of the car. I watched ahead. There were two semis ahead of us, but no cars. After we got to Schuyler, we didn't see the semis anymore. The radio said that no cars that got west of Schuyler that night, but we got through. When we got to Grand Island, the car got stuck in a ditch by the Burlington railroad underpass. A guy at the Ford garage helped us get it out and we made it home. We got back at four in the morning. We hadn't had any sleep. A lot of the streets had six, seven foot drifts. We wanted to get Etna to the hospital. In the morning the ambulance only got within two blocks of our house but they did get her to the hospital. The doctor told Etna that she had Hodgkin's disease.

Rosemarie, Deep Snow, Winter, 1948

In 1949, we went to Long Beach, California in our

green 1947 Chevrolet. My favorite car was that '47 Chevy that I bought in 1949. It was best car I ever had,

Warren's Green 1947 Chevrolet

but the '54 Ford owned by the City was the best car I ever drove. I drove the Chevy some 150,000 miles. The Chevy had belonged to the garage guy's wife who drove it back from Indiana. It cost $1300 or $1400. It didn't have many miles on it when I bought it. When it got 125,000 miles on it, I overhauled it myself.

On the way to California in 1949, we stayed over at Evanston, Wyoming. We also stayed in Las Vegas, Nevada. Then we went to Los Angeles and to Long Beach. In Long Beach, we stayed at the Beach-Shore Apartment Hotel by the Pacific Ocean where Marie's mother was working for a nurse who had nursed Marie when she was a baby. That's why we went there.

We saw a lot of things on our trip, we saw the second largest carrier ship at Redondo Beach. We saw Sunset Blvd. We visited friends in Glendale, California and went to the Forest Lawn Cemetery and Griffith's Park, ate dinner at Knottsberry Farm, we took a ride in the glass-bottom boat to Catalina Island. Lookout Mt. in San Francisco Bay and Sequoia National Park were very beautiful. I drove the Chevy on top of a fallen Redwood that had a man-made parking place on the top of it. Coming back, after we had been in San Francisco and Reno, we saw a dam in the Provo Mountains of Utah. Then we went on to Denver. We took Highway 70 through Kansas to Hastings, Nebraska. Then we came back home to Grand Island. We traveled 6,000 miles on that trip.

I took the family to California because I thought that it would be the last big trip we would take together as a family, and of course, it was.

ENDNOTES

1. Stacey Nerdin, "Great Oregon Waterfalls," 1997-1998 Robb and St. Online. Internet. Available: http://ucs.orst.edu/~nerdinr/Water.htm, April 7, 1999.

Chapter 6
1950-1959

Renewal and Change

By 1950, my job with the City had become routine. It was interesting and, sometimes, difficult, but it hadn't changed much since 1939 when I took over the country routes and started collecting for all the electric bills. The weather made my work hard sometimes. It would rain so hard at times that the dirt roads would be nothing but a sea of mud. I learned how to drive in it without getting stuck. In winter, I didn't like it when it got so bitter cold and the snow would get so deep and drift so badly that I couldn't get through. But, I got used to it. And I enjoyed the people. I liked to see what I could do to help if they had problems paying their bills.

Wally Kemp presenting a merit badge award to Rosemarie, 1952

One day in 1950, Marie and I came home from an outing and I found my mother-in-law, Rosa, downstairs. I told Marie, "Your Mom is downstairs. Go tell her to stay overnight." Marie went downstairs and talked a while with her mother. When she came back up, she told me, "Mom says you have a housekeeper." So I asked Marie, "Do you want her to stay here?" She said she did. So Rosa stayed here with us after that.

Rosemarie was still working in the Girl Scouts and earning merit badges all the time. She had so many badges that, in 1952, Wally Kemp gave her an award for merit badges. Wally was the Manager of the Capitol Theater and the Drive-In Theater. gave a merit badge award to Rosemarie for the Girl Scouts. Everyone liked Wally. He was always doing things for kids. Rosemarie had the second most Girl Scout badges in the United States. Only Debbie Reynolds had more badges at the time.

Our social life was as it always was. We went downtown on Saturday nights. We didn't miss many Saturday nights because that was Marie's life. It was her entertainment. We dropped in our folks as we did before, but we more often did not find people home. Most people had cars and they were gone half the time. More of the kids were growing up and getting married. People didn't sit on the front porch the way they used to.

Warren and Marie share a hug, Kuehner Farm, 1951

When she was old enough, I taught Rosemarie to

Chapter 6 - 1950-1959

Dick Kuehner, Bill, Bill Kuehner, Donald Steele, Rosemarie, 1952

drive the '47 Chevy. It had a stick shift and it took some getting used to. She took after me, I guess, and drove fast. A neighbor told me one day to tell her not to come down the street so fast. So I did and she slowed down a bit.

We got our first television in 1952. I bought it in a crate and took it home and set it up. I made myself an aerial for it and put it up. There was not much live television at first. We had a lot of old movies. We watched it a couple of hours in the evening. The television station at Holdredge was the only station that came in clear at first.

My sister Etna was losing the fight with cancer. She had Hodgkins disease. She had been sick with it for over 4 years. In 1953, she was in the hospital a lot and was losing ground all the time. The last week she was alive, I sat with her most of the time.

The closest I ever felt to God was when Etna died. The nurse put Etna's head in her hand and read to her from the Bible. She read the 23rd Psalm. Etna's eyes opened wide and were just as clear and sparkled. When the nurse finished her last words and removed her hand, Etna died.

In 1954, Rosemarie graduated from Grand Island high school. She was going to go Sioux Falls College in the fall. In the summer of 1954, Rosemarie was signed up to go to Colorado to work for the Girl Scouts as a camp counselor in training at the Flying G Ranch near Deckers in the mountains outside of Denver. It was a rugged camp and worked her hard, but she liked it. She went back to Flying G in the summer of 1955 and was a counselor.

In the fall of 1954, Rosemarie went to Sioux Falls College in Sioux Falls, South Dakota. When we took Rosemarie to Sioux Falls before she was to start college in 1954, we made it into a trip. We went to Chicago and up to Minneapolis and across Minnesota into North Dakota and then down to Sioux Falls. The Mississippi River up to Minneapolis from Chicago was so pretty; it is about the prettiest drive I've ever seen.

While Rosemarie was in college, I bet I made 15 trips to Sioux Falls. Nola Hudnall's mother from Chapman took Rosemarie up there a few times.

During this time, I probably made 50 short trips We saw quite a bit of country in that '47 Chevy. I put 150,000 miles on it.

In 1955, Rosemarie met Jim Skaine at Sioux Falls College. He was from the east. He had been born in Pennsylvania, but his folks were living in Buffalo, New York. They began to date and it wasn't long before they began to get serious about marriage.

In 1956, Sharon Ritchie, one of Rosemarie's high

school classmates, became Miss America.[1] That helped

Warren, Bill, Mom Skaine, Mom Keller, Wedding Dinner, Sioux Falls, June 1957

Grand Island receive the award as an All-American City. It was quite an honor.

In 1957, Grand Island had its centennial celebration. All men in Grand Island were required to grow beards. So when Rosemarie and Jim decided to get married, Bill and I had beards.

On June 4, 1957, Rosemarie married Jim. They wanted the wedding in Sioux Falls, so Marie, Bill and I went up there for it. I gave Rosemarie away at the wedding. Jim's mom, Ruth Skaine, came out from Buffalo for the wedding. She was a nice lady. I always liked her.

In April of 1958, my mother died in Oregon. When I heard that she had died, I called the Union Pacific to get a ticket to go out there. I was told that the train was full, that there were no tickets for me to buy.

I told them I was going to get on that train even if I had to stand all the way to the West Coast. I went down to the depot and was able to get a ticket. When I got on the train, there were only two or three other people in the car I was in. I thought it was strange they told me the train was filled and it turned out to be nearly empty.

In June 1958, Rosemarie earned her B.A. degree in sociology from the University of South Dakota in Vermillion. Jim earned his M.A. degree in speech at the same time. Jim was offered a job as a graduate assistant at Cornell University in Ithaca, New York to work on his PhD in speech. Rosemarie wanted to keep working in Girl Scouts so she applied to work for the Scouts in Ithaca. She was offered a job as an assistant to the woman in charge of the Scouts. She accepted it. They were getting ready to go to Ithaca when they got word that the woman who hired her was

Warren and Rosemarie, June 4, 1957

killed in a car crash. The Girl Scout organization in Ithaca decided they didn't want to hire anybody until they got a new person hired, so they told Rosemarie, she didn't have a job. When Rosemarie and Jim went to Ithaca, Rosemarie found a job teaching English in a school in Ovid, New York, which is 26 miles north of Ithaca.

In 1958, the roof of my house got hailed off. I put a new roof on myself. My insurance man called me and asked if I was going to put in for insurance. I said I hadn't thought about it. He said I should put in for it. I did and I got paid for the roof.

I took the money I got for the roof and went east with Marie and Bill in July 1959. We went in my 1952 Ford. We went first to see Rosemarie and Jim in Ithaca. Then we all decided go to New York City. We stayed there a couple of days and had a lot of fun . We ate once at a place where you put your money in a slot, then opened a little door, and got your food. Marie thought that was quite something. We went to the Statue of Liberty and to the Coney Island Amusement Park. We went to Coney Island because we were in the subway and a train came by that said, "Coney Island," so we got on it. I sure enjoyed Coney Island. Not long after that they tore Coney Island down and built apartments. They tore it down in the '60s.

When I was on the trip to New York, my Dad died in Oregon. I didn't find out that he died until I returned to Grand Island. I wasn't able to attend his funeral.

ENDNOTES

1. http://missamerica.org/missamericas/1956.html, August 24 1998. Online. Internet. Available: Feb. 15, 1999.

Chapter 7
1960-1969

New Lives and New Directions

The transforming 1950s passed into the turbulent 1960s. The 1960s saw three leaders fall from an assassin's bullet: President John F. Kennedy, Robert Kennedy, the President's brother and Attorney General of the U.S., and Martin Luther King, Jr., famed Black civil rights leader. In addition, President Kennedy's assassin, Lee Harvey Oswald, was shot and killed by Jack Ruby. President Lyndon Johnson succeeded Kennedy and instituted the Civil Rights Act of 1964.

The 1960s brought the personal life changes for me including changes of life and death.

I worked with the Boys Scouts in Grand Island as I had done for years. I was involved in many of the troop's activities. I was treasurer for the troop for years. In 1961, they gave me an award for having worked with them twenty years.

On September 15, 1961, I became a grandfather. Rosemarie and Jim had a boy. They named him James Keller Skaine, but they called him Jimmy. He was born while Rosemarie and Jim were still in Ithaca. In 1960, Jim had started work as an instructor at Ithaca College.

At Christmas, Rosemarie and Jim brought Jimmy to Grand Island. They had quite a time on the way out. They got stuck in a blizzard near Des Moines, Iowa and some kind people in Mitchellville, Iowa took them in and put them up.

Marie and Camille Marie Skaine, Murfreesboro, Tennessee, 1963

The next year, they had another child. This time it was a girl. On November 21, 1962, Camille Marie Skaine was born.

In 1962, my mother in law, Rosa Kuehner, got cancer and died. She had lived with us for many of the last years of her life.

In May 1963, I-80 was completed south of Grand Island. It was a four lane divided highway. It wouldn't be many years before I-80 would stretch from the east coast to the west. Interstates were a far cry from the trails that I followed when I was driving around the country when I was working for the bridge gang. The new roads were nice, but I still liked to travel the other roads. I would take Highway 30 places instead of the interstate. I liked to go through small towns and eat at the restaurants along the way. When I was on the interstate, it just wasn't as interesting.

In 1963, Rosemarie and Jim moved to Murfreesboro, Tennessee where Jim was hired as an assistant professor at Middle Tennessee State College. That fall,

Chapter 7 - 1960-1969

Marie, Bill and I went to visit them in Murfreesboro. I had bought a 1962 Ford Coupe just before we went. Murfreesboro was about 35 miles outside of Nashville. On Saturday night, Marie, Bill, Rosemarie and I went to the Grand Ole Opry in Nashville. I had always wanted to see it. I'd listened to the Opry since I got my first radio in 1928.

In 1964, on August 25, Camille Marie took ill quite suddenly and died. She had meningitis. She was a sweet little girl.

In 1965, I retired from the City. I had worked for them for forty years to the day. I began working there on May 5, 1925 at noon and retired at noon on May 5, 1965. I didn't want to quit, but it was the law. The federal government made me quit. They gave me a dinner and a gift when I retired.

I miss the people I came across in my work. I was always interested in people. As a kid, I'd hear people say they were going to do something, then they didn't. I began to wonder why they didn't do what they said they would. So I took to trying to figure people out.

Warren and Marie at Warren's retirement dinner, 1965

I liked my work. I always got along with people. In the early days when I was collecting, times were tough. People paid when they had it. I never had to ask people to pay their bill. They knew they owed it and they paid. In my work, I had to go inside people's houses to read the meters. People trusted me. Some people gave me the key to their house because they weren't going to be home.

I did a lot of listening to troubles. Most people were sincere. One day a lady called my boss and complained. Clarence Burdick asked me why. "Well," I said, "I didn't have time to listen to all of her stories today." The boss didn't say any more.

Warren receiving a gift from Frank Phelps at his retirement, Marie, Mrs. Andy Kosh, and Mr. Andy Kosh, May 1965

One lady was always offering me a couple beers. I always said no. I had to be careful, because she wanted me not to collect her money. Another woman ran a restaurant and had a home to take care of. She couldn't pay. I could have had her lights shut off, but then she would never be able to pay. So I didn't shut them off, and in about four months, she was able to pay.

One day, my boss, Burdick, said to me, "Somebody called in and said your car was parked all afternoon in front of such and such a place." I said, "Well,

Chapter 7 - 1960-1969

did they also tell you that I read meters all afternoon to west of the 1700 block?" "Well, park it somewhere else next time,' Burdick said. Burdick never mentioned it anymore.

In 1965, Jim took a job as an assistant professor of speech at the State College of Iowa in Cedar Falls. In the summer before he was to start, they went back to Ithaca to have Jim do more graduate work at Cornell. In August, they had another child. Forrest Todd Skaine was born on August 7. He was three weeks old when they moved to Cedar Falls.

After I quit the City, I went to work on a city parking lot. The parking lot that was for people doing business with the stores around. It cost 15 cents an hour to park. The business people had a stamp. If customers bought stuff, the merchants would let them park free.

Then I worked in the parking lot for the bank. I made sure that the bank customers had a place to park and that those who were not bank customers would not park there. At times, business was slow, so I would read. While I worked at the Bank, I read the Bible three times. That's when I commenced to learn what I was here for. I defined myself when I read the Bible those three times.

In December of 1968, I got a lifetime certificate of membership in the Sons and Daughters of the Soddies. It was signed by the president, V. A. Kear. I was glad to get it because it reminded me of when I was a young kid and when I was around sod houses. The

certificate said,
>"Born in
>Attended Churches
>Lived in a Sod House
>Helped Build Sod Houses

Todd Skaine, Bill Keller, Jimmy Skaine, Grand Island, 1969

In 1969, the bank didn't need an attended parking lot anymore so I was out of a job. I was home one day and the Commercial Bank called and asked me to take care of some of their paperwork that they usually had college kids do. I said I would and went to work for them.

Chapter 8
1970-1979

Growth and Loss

In 1970, I was working at the Bank. I was no longer working in the parking lot. I did other jobs like take money from one bank to another and pick up paper work at one branch and take it to another.

Bill's health was getting worse all the time. He couldn't do much work at all. He drove his car, but he was not able to go far in it. He had collected coins for some time and now got more involved with it. Marie took good care of Bill. She made sure that he had his treatments and took his medicine.

In May of 1971, the last passenger train went through Grand Island. I remember when I tried to get a ticket to go to my mother's funeral in 1958. Even then, the railroads didn't want passengers. They made more money hauling freight. I missed the trains when they stopped running. I enjoyed the rides that I'd taken on the train to Oregon.

One evening in the early '70s, Marie and I were sitting in the living room watching television when we heard a loud pop. One of the bulbs in the lamp exploded. Lightning had hit a little aerial on the roof that I had up there for Bill's radio. It hit that and burned it up. It knocked one side of the line out, but it didn't affect the one to the television. I asked Marie if she was all right. She said she was, but she looked stunned.

Afterwards she said she may have answered me but she didn't remember it.

The lightning did most of the damage downstairs. It went through the phone and every screw on the furnace and air conditioner was black. I had my neighbor Richard Franzen call the fire department. It was smoking. The fire department found Bill's television burning. The lightning fixed it for good. We still could watch television because it didn't come in on that side of the line. It burned the telephone wires to the alley. It was a long time before I got the telephone service back.

In 1973, my eyesight acted up. I had a cataract growing on my right eye. I went to old Dr. Proffitt and he said he could remove it. He removed the cornea when he operated on it. That's the way they did it in those days. After that, I had to wear a contact lens in order not to see double.

In 1974, Rosemarie went to work for the University as the departmental secretary in the Sociology Department at the University of Northern Iowa. It wasn't long before she started to work on getting an M.A. degree.

In 1975, some of the trees in my back yard I had planted in the 1940s had seen their best days and needed to come down. Marie's brother, Bill Kuehner and his sons, Bill and Dick, came over to help. My nephew Bill tells it this way. "Dad came to town with a front loader. Dad lifted me high. We did our sawing with a chain saw. When a tree fell, we yelled for Warren to pull with the truck that was attached by cable to the tree. When Warren pulled, the tree twisted on the way down and fell on his neighbor's roof, breaking the TV antenna and phone line, and destroying some shingles. We spent considerable time making repairs to the neighbor's roof. Another tree fell on the North side. We removed the air

Warren and Marie, 50th Wedding Anniversary, December 23, 1976

conditioner so that wouldn't break. Warren climbed up the tree like a monkey, 40 feet high. We yelled, 'What are you doing in the tree?' He was only 75 at the time!

There was a cable in the tree. The tree twisted and hit the 2 x 12s on the air conditioner and hit the utility power line and broke the utility pole in the alley . Warren knew some people at the Utilities. The pole was rotten. Warren probably saved someone's life."

I guess those trees weren't meant to come down easy. I was glad for the help. And I was glad that those trees were out of there.

On December 23, 1976, Marie and I celebrated our 50th wedding anniversary. We held it at the Kuehner homestead, where Marie grew up. Rosemarie and Carolyn Kuehner arranged for it. Marie and I had seen much of life in those 50 years. We had had a lot of good times.

In 1977, Marie's brother, Bill, and his wife, Frieda, had their 50th wedding anniversary. Marie and

Bill and Frieda Kuehner, 50th Wedding Anniversary, 1977

I had a lot of good times over the years with Bill and

Chapter 8 - 1970-1979

Frieda.

After Thanksgiving in 1978, Marie didn't seem like herself. I thought she was coming down with something serious. Finally, in January of 1979, I took her to the doctor. The doctor said she had leukemia and that we should have her taken to University Hospital in Omaha because it was the best in the state. She went there by ambulance. I followed the ambulance in my Plymouth. It was a powerful car. I drove 100 mph and barely kept up with the ambulance.

The doctors in Omaha said Marie had leukemia and said that she should get treated. She was in Omaha several weeks for treatments. She then came back to Grand Island. Later, she went back to Omaha and got a second series of treatments. She came back here to Grand Island, but she wasn't doing so well so they took her to Lutheran Hospital in Grand Island.

The last day of May, I went to the hospital to see Marie. I took one look at her and knew that she didn't have long to live. I called her brother, Bill, and Frieda and said, "Marie is not doing so good. You'd best come if you want to see her alive."

They came. We were with Marie when she died. It was late afternoon. She was sitting in a chair. She leaned back and quit breathing. I sent the nurse in there and then went and called Rosemarie.

Rosemarie says, "I remember that day, May 31, vividly. Working late, the phone interrupted my mundane routine thoughts. 'Rosemarie,' a familiar voice said, 'This is your Dad. Your mother passed away at 8:00 this evening.' I'm sure he and I said more, but I do not remember any more of the conversation. Her death was expected, but the reality, for me, was very difficult.

"My son, Jimmy, found his Grandmother's death difficult. Jimmy had just graduated from Cedar Falls High School. In a most meaningful conversation, Jimmy and I discussed the pastoral message at my mother's funeral. Life is filled with graduations, the minister explained. If we can view death as a graduation into God's Kingdom of Eternal Life rather than as something irretrievably final, then we will have an easier time accepting death for the happy celebration that God intended. Jimmy, just having graduated from high school, found new meaning in the word graduate.

"For me, my Uncle Bill Kuehner helped. At the lunch after her funeral, I watched my Uncle, standing not far from me, in a tender moment, reach up and, with the palm of his hand, wipe a tear. I walked over to him. I do not recall what I said to him, but I shall never forget his words of wisdom, 'Death is part of life, Rosie.' Common sense has a way of eluding us sometimes, but Uncle Bill gently and kindly brought it back for me. Mother loved her brothers.

"My father helped me move on with life by moving on with his own in his princely manner. A moment I shall not forget came as we pulled out of the driveway to return to Cedar Falls. My father stood, a solitary figure on the front porch of the only home I had ever known growing up, and waved. Later I would talk to him and he told me that he returned to the cemetery alone that day, perhaps to say his last most personal goodbye."

One of my favorite cars was the Maroon 1980 Mercury. I bought it in 1979, after Marie died. I debated whether to buy it and decided to do it. It was a good car. I put 55,000 miles on it.

Chapter 9
1980-1989

Loss and Good Friends

In 1980, Bill's health kept getting worse. He asked me if we could to fly to Oregon to see the folks out there. I said I'd go if the doctor said it was okay. The doctor said that Bill couldn't stand the high altitudes that planes fly at. A trip like that might kill him. So we didn't go.

Ruby Loop would call Bill to see how he was. She had always been a good friend of the family. We'd known her since 1924. When Marie was in the hospital the last time, Ruby would go see her every day. Marie looked forward to her being there. She'd say, "Is Ruby coming?" She always brightened up when Ruby was around. After Marie died, Ruby looked out for Bill.

Ruby Loop

In May of 1980, Bill and I took a trip in the 1980 Mercury. We couldn't go to Oregon, so we did the next best thing. We traveled through Missouri, Illinois and Iowa and ended up at Rosemarie and Jim's place in Cedar Falls. We had to cut short our stay in Cedar Falls because Bill began to get sicker.

Not long after we got home, Grand Island was hit by tornadoes. On June 3, 1980, tornadoes damaged a lot of the city and killed some people. The *Independent* said that five were dead and that $300 million in damages had been done. The series of tornadoes destroyed 475 living units and 49 businesses.

Jim Skaine in his office at the University of Northern Iowa

After those tornadoes hit, Grand Island was a war zone. You couldn't go anyplace because of the downed trees. Right north of us, one tornado pulled a bunch of big cottonwood trees up by the roots. East of us, it turned a house around, that's how close it got to me. There were seven tornadoes, up around the Soldiers' Home, down on south Locust, 10th and Sycamore, and other places. Our power went out. I was without lights for a week. Bill had to have that machine for his lungs. I had just put a half of beef in the deep freeze, so I had to get a generator. I went around town until I found one. It would run out of gas about four in the morning, so I had to keep it going for Bill and the deep freeze. We used a candle for light."

I read in the *Independent* that many people were unaware of the ruin left by as many as seven tornadoes that had twisted and blown their way slowly through the

Chapter 9 - 1980-1989

heart of Grand Island.[1] It said that the last tornado struck on South Locust around 10:30 P.M. Other twisters extensively damaged the Nebraska Veteran's

Tornado Damage, South Locust Street, June 1980

Home and Veteran's Administration Hospital. Patients were safely evacuated to the basement. The next day, when people came out of their basements, they were unaware of the extensive damage.

The tornadoes just about finished Bill. He got worse after that. He'd go over to the store, three and a half blocks away. It would take him a good hour to go over there on foot. The clerks were good to him.

In the middle of July, I told Bill I was going to quit my job. I had told him, "I'm not going to work anymore. I'm going to stay here with you." Before I could do that, Bill got worse. I said to Doc Anderson, "We're fighting a losing battle." Anderson said get him to the hospital.

A couple days later, I came home from the hospital and Bill called me. He tried to tell me something three times, but didn't have enough air. Finally, he gave up. Within an hour, the nurse called and said that I should get back over there. Bill was dead when I got back to the hospital. He died of emphysema on Saturday, July 19, 1980.

Ruby was there for me after Bill died. We began to see each other. We were good for each other.

In 1981, I told the bank that I was going to go to Oregon and if they wanted, I would give them my notice. After a couple of days, they called me in and said they wanted me to stay and gave me a nickel an hour raise.

I had a little problem with my heart in 1982, I told the doctor that "I guess I'll just retire." I was going to try to make it to 20 years of work after I retired from the City. The doc said, "good." I retired for good in 1983.

In December of 1983, I had my left eye operated on for cataracts. This time, the younger Dr. Proffitt operated on me. He did what he called a cornea implant. He told me I would not have to wear a contact lens on this eye. It was amazing how much progress had been made since my first eye operation.

In the early '80s, I had my neighbor to the west, Richard Franzen, build a garage for me. I built the

Chapter 9 - 1980-1989

biggest garage I could, but because the house was 4 feet too close to the property line, I didn't have room for a double garage. After I built it, I had a conversation with Rosemarie about why I did it. Rosemarie says, "At the time, I couldn't figure my father out. Here was a great outdoor man, a confirmed tinkerer, and a very skilled driver, electing to put his car in a garage. Why, I asked myself, did he no longer want to put a heater that was on the end of an extension cord, under the hood overnight. Then one day, he said, 'You know, I just love to scrape the frost off the windshield in the morning on a cold day, and I'm a gonna' miss that, but this way if somethin' would happen, they can't say, 'Old fool, didn't even have his windows clean. No wonder.' The windows would be just as clean as if I'd done them by hand, but you gotta' be a step ahead of society as you get older. Aging is largely attitudinal.'"

In 1985, Howard and Colleen Maxon moved next door to me to the west at 416 West 16th. Howard says, "In October of 1985, it was quite a day moving in. Warren had a red Mercury with a stick shift. He was leaning on the red car in the driveway. We were unloading boxes when he came over and said, 'Keller's the name, Warren.' We could tell he was going to be a good neighbor."

Less than a year later, Howard needed me to watch his house while he was at the hospital with his wife. Howard says, "On August 14, 1986 we had a fire in our house. Colleen was having a baby and I was with her at the hospital. We had planned on having a quiet birth event. The phone rang at the hospital in the room we were in and it was the 911 center informing us that the house was on fire. Warren had come home for the day and heard paint cans exploding in our basement. Upon investigating further, Warren noticed that there was smoke coming out around the windows and doors of our house. I later listened to the 911 tape recording of Warren reporting the fire. If it hadn't been for Warren, the fire would have caused a lot more damage. As it was, the fire was so hot that it melted solder on a water pipe and the pipe fell in such a position to actually shoot water at the fire."

In December 1987, I bought a 1988 Ford Taurus. I bought it in Kearney at Crossroads Ford from Howard's father. I sure hated to give up the Mercury, but it acted up and I couldn't depend on it. It would slow down and go into idle for a while and then it would be all right. They couldn't find how to fix it, so I sold it.

In 1988, the contact lens in my right eye began acting up. The eye I had operated on in 1973. I couldn't have it in for long until it began to hurt. So I told Rosemarie about it and she said that there was a real good eye clinic in Marshalltown, Iowa, the Wolf Eye Clinic, that had a branch in Cedar Falls. So I agreed to have my eye looked at. In September, I went with Rosemarie and Jim to Marshalltown and the doctor who examined me, Dr. Woodlief, said that I was a candidate for an implant. I asked, "When can we do it?" He said next week in

Chapter 9 - 1980-1989

Cedar Falls. So I went to the hospital in Cedar Falls and they did the operation in the morning and I went home in the afternoon. I had a patch over my eye and had to sleep a certain way. After a couple of days, I wanted to go home to Grand Island. I knew the doctor told me to be back in two weeks for a checkup, but I wanted to be in Grand Island. We called the doctor and he said he didn't advise me to go but that, if I wanted to, it was up to me. So I drove the 400 miles back to Grand Island. When it came time for the checkup, I drove back to Cedar Falls. The checkup went fine. The doctor said I didn't have to wear the patch anymore. After I saw the doctor, I drove back to Grand Island. I had driven 1600 miles to get my eye fixed, but it was worth it.

Later that fall, Rosemarie, Jim and I were looking at some old pictures I had of my relatives. They thought it would be nice to take some of the pictures, have copies made and then put them all together in a frame. When they came to Grand Island at Christmas, they brought the picture with them. I read the title. It said, "The Warren V. Keller Heritage, A Sketch in Pictures." It had my mother and father, my grandmother Jinks and my great-grandmother Amsberry. It had Marie and her mother and father. Bill, Rosemarie and Jim and the grandchildren. And it had Ruby Loop. I told them, "I believe this picture is the nicest gift you have ever given me."

Rosemarie says, "The picture brought forth many interesting conversations about life in yesteryear.

Basically, men were the boss outside of the home, and women were inside of the home. But how different life styles were between some men and some women probably weren't all that different from today. My father told me of a relative, a single woman, who lived not far from his family. The woman loved children. A man who worked near by, 'helped her get her babies,' Dad said.

I said, 'So this type of male-female relationship is comparable to a single woman, today, who desires to be a single parent. The most high profile case today is Madonna.' So, if you think about my Dad, and try to figure out why he is very perceptive and can understand life today, it is most likely because he was and is very observant and has always been tolerant."

Howard, John Whyte, my neighbor to the east, and I always had a lot of fun. John says, "When Warren was 89 years old, he was mowing Howard's lawn because Howard had gone on vacation." The pic-

Warren mowing Howard's lawn as it appeared in the *Independent*

ture ended up in the *Independent*. Howard told us, "You know I kind of got razzed about that."

Howard says that one time he was fooled when he checked on me in his usual way. Howard says, "In the mornings I always looked out the kitchen window when I got up to see if Warren had a light on in the kitchen. I could see through a crack in the shade off to the side. When daylight came, Warren always put the shade up. One day, the shade stayed down and I became worried. My worries were soon calmed when I called over to Ruby's and found that Warren was there. I started to explain to Ruby about no light and the shade was down. Ruby turned away from the phone and hollered at Warren, 'Honey, you forgot to put up your shade.'"

I had a cordless phone before many people had one. Soon after, Ruby got one. One day I was fixing Ruby's phone and called Howard over to help. When Howard got there he sized it up this way. "Warren is good at fixing things and Ruby was having a problem with her cordless phone. Warren asked me to come over to Ruby's to see if I could help him fix her phone. When I got there, Ruby, Warren and two of Ruby's daughters were all sitting in the living room of Ruby's apartment. I worked with the phone for a while and then suggested that Warren take Ruby's cordless phone home and bring his to Ruby, then see if the problem followed the phone or stayed with the location. I figured interference in Ruby's neighborhood may have been the problem. I received puzzled looks on the faces of all but Warren's.

Then one of Ruby's daughters looked at me and said, 'But if Warren takes Mama's phone home, Mama's calls will go to Warren's house. Mama needs her calls here!' Warren and I exchanged smiles and the look on Warren's face said 'Ain't that the damnedest thing you ever heard?'"

Howard says, "Warren has always been up on technology. He had a better TV and stereo than I did. One day he called on the telephone and asked me to come over and look at his TV. 'What's it doing?' I asked. He said that the sound that was coming out of the speaker on the TV didn't have anything to do with the picture. I told Colleen that I thought Warren had lost it. So, I went over to Warren's to check the TV. When I came home I told Colleen, 'Warren's right. What is coming out of the speaker doesn't have anything to do with the picture.' Later we discovered that Warren was watching the educational television network and had the bilingual button turned on. On ETV the bilingual sound channel has the talking book for the blind. We hit the button and the sound matched the picture.

"In 1989 I renewed my interest in ham radio. I had been talking on the radio to other hams in other states when the phone rang. I answered and Warren calmly said 'Howard?' and then his pace picked up rather fast. 'What the hell is going on? There is talking in my stereo and it sounds like Donald Duck.' My ham radio was interfering with his stereo so I got the parts needed to put on his stereo and that cleared up the

Chapter 9 - 1980-1989

problem."

Howard's kids would come over to my house. One time, John came over. I didn't know why he was there but Howard told me later. "My son John got mad at me one day and announced that he was going to run away. I suggested to him the things that he might need and suggested that he pack a grocery sack for what he will need. He said goodbye to me and left with his sack. I watched to see where he went. I figured that he would go to Chuck and Mary McBrides, his babysitter. He went to Warren's front door and rang the doorbell. Warren greeted him at the door and let him in. It wasn't long and the back doorbell rang at our house and I answered it. It was John and he said, 'Hi dad, it sure is good to be back home.' Later I talked to Warren about what he and John discussed. Warren said John asked him if he had any toys, any videos or did he have cable tv? Warren answered to that was no to all three. John then told Warren that he was going home."

I had a good family, good friends and good neighbors. I was fortunate.

ENDNOTES

1. Night of the Twisters: The 1980 Tornadoes, The Day After, *The Grand Island Independent.* Online. Internet. Available: Twisters @ theIndependent.com: The day after 10/08/98. Accessed: 4/6/1999.

Chapter 10
1990-1999

Near Death and Ongoing Life

1990 was a year when my heart acted up on me. In July, Howard Maxon found me lying in the driveway. I had been mowing the lawn, and my heart got out of rhythm. Howard says, "We came home one noon and Warren had gotten sick. There he was lying in his drive. I told Colleen to go in and call an ambulance, and I went over and talked to Warren. He was able to talk to me. I told him everything will be O.K. and to take deep breaths. When the ambulance guys arrived, I introduced Warren to them, 'This is Warren Keller; he is a pretty tough guy.'"

I ended up in the hospital that time, but was out in a couple of days. Later, in October, I drove to Cedar Falls to see Rosemarie and Jim. I was there a couple of days and then left in the morning to drive home. I stopped on the way to see a friend in Shenandoah, Iowa. Then I came home a little after dark. For the life of me, the only thing I remember about that trip was standing by the side of the road at a rest area as I was going south on Interstate 29 out of Des Moines.

On election day in November, I voted and then I cleaned the snow off the driveways and walks for my place and for Howard and John Whyte, my neighbor to the East. As, John tells it, "I had just had an operation. Warren was shoveling snow on Election Day. I looked out the door and told him to let it go, but he said, 'Oh, I'll just do this little bit.' Well, he did the whole thing. So I said, 'Come in and have some coffee.' So, Warren sat on the north side of the kitchen table, and I sat on the west side and poured him a cup of coffee. Warren leaned straight over and fell all the way down. I didn't have very much wind, I had just had an operation, so, Rosie loosened up his shirt collar to see if he was still breathing.

"John had CPR training," Rosie said, "A young man from Blessed Sacrament just happened to come to the door. John answered the door. Then John asked him if he knew CPR and he said no. So John asked him to call 911. So, he did. The ambulance arrived in about two minutes. John wanted to get down there, but I said no, because then we'd have two people in trouble. I had seen CPR administered on TV. I didn't leave Warren's side. I felt for a pulse after loosening his collar and started blowing into his mouth."

"The medics didn't say hello or anything. They shoved the table out of the way," John adds.

"I'd never seen medics at work. The paddles to get his heart started didn't work at first. They had to use them more than once," Rosie said.

"Warren jumped way off the floor," John said.

"The medics grabbed my pills off the table," Rosie said, "I said, 'Hey, those are my pills.' Then they asked whether I knew what medication Warren was taking."

Howard Maxon said, "I heard the call over 911.

Chapter 10 - 1990-1999

I was at work when the call came in. The 911 center supervisor came into my office to tell me what had happened. He said, 'It does not sound good.' I just knew it was the end. To my surprise, Warren made it to St. Francis hospital and was doing good. I went up to see him and he knew who I was. I thought I would see if he knew a few other things so I asked him the date and year, and he gave them correctly. I asked if he remembered that his wife had passed on and he said in a very concerned voice, 'No, I don't remember that.' I then asked if he knew that his son, Bill, had passed on and he said, 'Yes, I know that.'"

I wasn't aware of what happened until days later. Some of what happened I never remembered, but each day, I began to remember more. I was in the hospital a week and then came home. Dr. Cannella told me I had not had a heart attack, but my heart had gotten out of rhythm so bad that it had stopped. He said it was cardiac arrest. He prescribed some medicine for me and I have had to take it since.

If John hadn't called me into the house for a cup of coffee, I don't think I would be alive today. I would have gone home and my heart would have acted up and nobody would have been around to know. "By the grace of God," Rosie said, "It was meant for Warren to have some more time earth."

Howard said, "After this incident, Pastor John Russell, our pastor at St. Pauls Lutheran, talked to me and said that he had told Warren that he should not be scooping snow and asked me to reinforce that. So, I went over to Warren's and took his snow scoops away and told him that I would take care of the snow from now on. One day, Warren called me up on the phone and said, 'Boy, do I have a deal for you.' I said, "O.K.? Warren said, 'I'll buy the snow blower and you run it!' I said, 'You got a deal.' Warren got a kick out of running the snow blower so he did some of the snow work himself. Many times after a big snow it is sun shiny and not so cold, so I guess he thought he could do that. One day I came home from work and he had blown all my snow. The next day there was a story in the newspaper about him blowing my snow and they quoted Warren as saying, 'That way when Howard comes home he can rest.' Warren probably knew that I had left in the wee hours of the morning to go to work to coordinate emergency things with the blizzard."

Ruby and I were still seeing each other. Howard Maxon says,"Warren and Ruby used to sit out under the oak tree in Warren's back yard. Warren had a swinging kind of a love seat that they sat in."

Howard looked after me. Howard says, "In the mornings when I got up, I'd look over at the crack in the shade in Warren's kitchen window to see if he had a light on. Monday was wash day. When Ruby was able, she was over there at five or six in the morning to do the laundry. I heard her sometimes. She'd be out in the driveway, whistling and drinking a cup of coffee. When Ruby couldn't do the wash anymore, and it was Monday,

Chapter 10 - 1990-1999

Warren came home with a sack over his shoulder. I kind of think Monday was still wash day, only Warren was doing the washing."

Ruby's health was not good on more days now. She had an enlarged heart that kept her from doing what she used to. She didn't want to slow down and sometimes would overdo. She had a knee that acted up and was operated on. Most of the time if she went out, I'd have to wheel her to the car in a wheelchair she had. To make it easier for her to get around, we bought an electric cart. She would go all over Pletcher Terrace with it.

In 1993, I decided that I would not again drive in my own car from Grand Island to Cedar Falls to visit Rosemarie and Jim. Rosemarie says, "That Dad could and would take the eight hour drive up to that time is, in and of itself, a marvel. Many who were younger at the time, could not sit behind the wheel of a car for eight hours straight with only a stop to fill up the gas tank. Often, Dad did not stop for a coffee break or restroom break." I figured I could still drive around town and in the country a ways. I had done a lot of that in the past. I figure I had driven a car within 5 to 15 miles of Grand Island, many years, around 18 to 20 thousand miles a year.

In April 1993, I planned to go to Oregon to see Twila and Wally. They were married in 1933, so April 19th would have been their 60th anniversary. I was going to fly out there and help them celebrate it. On

April 12, Twila had a heart attack and passed away. I went to Oregon, but it was to attend a memorial not to celebrate an anniversary. Twila was the last of my folks to die. Rosemarie is the only family I have left.

In 1994, Rosemarie, Jim and I began talking about taking a trip back east. I had always wanted to visit the places my mother and father were born. She was born in Southside, West Virginia and he was born in New Amsterdam, Indiana. I wanted to get back to my roots.

My dad's people had moved to Indiana from the Shenandoah Valley in Virginia and I wanted to see that area, too. As a boy, I was curious about my Grandfather Jinks. When I was growing up, no one ever talked about him. I knew his name was William Robert Jinks, but that was about all. My Grandmother Jinks had come to Mason City after he died and had married Nick Peterson. So Nick Peterson was the grandfather on my mother's side that I knew. As a kid, I wondered if Grandfather Jinks had been a gambler or had done something people were ashamed of. I learned that he was buried in Viers Chapel Cemetery in Southside.

We decided to go. Before we left Cedar Falls, I had some question about going. Rosemarie says, "A conversation Dad and I had prior to the trip is probably the most heart rending of all our talks. Dad came to stay with us in Cedar Falls a couple days before we left on the trip. One day he was riding my aero-dyne bicycle. Over the roar of the bike, he kept mumbling. I approached the bike and asked, 'Dad, what is it you are

Chapter 10 - 1990-1999

trying to say?' He stopped pedaling. Quiet prevailed. His eyes reflected a sadness I did not understand. 'What will you do with me in D.C.?' he asked. 'Do with you? What do you mean, what will I do with you?' 'You won't know what to do if I get sick or something.' 'Well, yes, I will,' I said firmly, launching into steps I would take should it become necessary. Ending upbeat, I said, 'But we are going into this trip with the attitude that you won't be ill; that you will be well.' 'Yes, but,' his downcast eyes looked up, 'I mean like what if you have to put me in a box or something.' Speechless, I looked into his unrelenting eyes. 'Oh, Daddy,' I said. Moved by the tenderness of the moment, I hugged him."

Rosemarie and Warren at the gate of the Keller Homestead, 1994

In late May, 1994, we flew to Washington, D.C.

I had never been there. Rosemarie was working on her first book and wanted to do some research in Washington. We drove out to Tom's Brook, Virginia in the Shenandoah Valley to the Keller homestead . The Kellers and Hottels had moved there in the 1750s. When the Shenandoah Valley became crowded, some moved to the west and that is why my father was born in Indiana.

We drove out of Tom's Brook, looking for the Keller Homestead. We ran into the Hottel-Keller Cemetery. We visited that awhile and then went on to the Keller Homestead. Rosemarie says, "Once in the back yard, I stood behind my father as he looked over the Blue Ridge mountains. Dressed in casual slacks as was his genteel custom, complete with a summer hat atop his head, he raised his right hand, 'Why now, this is what I like. It's so peaceful.' That it was, even for me. But for him, the peace of being in the mountains returned to him the peaceful solace he knew as a young boy working in the hills around Mason City, Nebraska."

After we visited the Keller Homestead, we went back to Washington. Rosemarie had to get back to Cedar Falls to work. On Sunday, Jim and I

Keller Homestead near Tom's Brook, VA., 1994

Chapter 10 - 1990-1999

flew from Washington Dulles Airport to Charleston, West Virginia. We rented a car and started out. It was Sunday afternoon when we got there and so we decided to drive to Indiana first and then come back to Southside. We stayed overnight in Lexington, Kentucky and drove to New Amsterdam on Memorial Day morning. New Amsterdam is just across the Ohio River from Kentucky and is not far from Louisville. After visiting New Amsterdam, we headed to Southside. Jim asked if I wanted to go to Indianapolis and to see the Indianapolis Speedway, where they had raced the Indianapolis 500 on Sunday. I said I did and so we went to Indianapolis. I had always wanted to see the Speedway. It sure is big.

Warren riding in a cart, going up to Viers Chapel Cemetery

We left Indianapolis, but we knew we wouldn't make it to West Virginia that day. We stayed in Indiana overnight and the next day we headed for Southside. We drove though Cincinnati and then east through Ohio to Southside, West Virginia. When we got to Southside, we stopped and asked directions to the Viers Chapel Cemetery. Jim describes our visit, "We headed into the hills along a winding road and found ourselves at the home of Floyd Stuart. The man at the grain elevator who gave us directions told us that the road up to Viers Chapel was not passable by car. Floyd Stuart told us that he took care of the cemetery and he was planning to go up there anyway to take some of the Memorial Day flags down. Floyd Stuart drove his tractor and we rode in the cart up to the cemetery. Dad Keller rode standing up and holding on to the sides of the cart."

In January 1995, for my 95th birthday, Howard and Colleen gave me a card party. I received 116 cards

Warren looking at his 116 birthday cards he received for his 95th birthday

in all. Colleen says of the event, "He started out with a little table to stand his cards on, so that people could see them. Some more cards came so he said, 'I guess I'd better put up the card table,' but even more cards came.

Chapter 10 - 1990-1999

He just kind of gave up on tables, and put them all on the floor." Howard says, "In 1995, when we gave Warren a birthday card shower, we put an announcement in the newspaper that read, '"Sakes alive, Warren Keller turned 95.' Warren received over 100 cards. When I asked him about the cards and whether he remembered the people who sent them, he replied 'I even got some cards from people that I thought were dead.'

In 1995, Rosemarie, Jim and I talked about going back to Virginia to attend the Hottel-Keller Reunion. We also talked about going to Southside again. We had made contact with Irene and Rod Brand who live in Southside . They were distant relatives and both knew a lot about the Beard and Amsberry families. Rod had dug up some records in the county courthouse and found that my Grandfather Jinks had been born just across the Ohio River in Ohio and that he was a lawyer when he died of tuberculosis in December 1888. Irene and Rod said they would take us to the Amsberry and Beard places around Southside if we came back.

In August 1995, Rosemarie, Jim and I flew to Washington a second time. Rosemarie was still researching her book. Two retired Navy lawyers, Rear Admirals John E. "Ted" Gordon and Duvall M. "Mac" Williams, Jr. invited all of us to lunch at the historic Army and Navy Club in Washington, D.C. That was quite an honor.

When we were at the family reunion, I was asked to give a speech. As Rosemarie tells it, "Minutes before his family reunion supper and before his speech, Dad said to me, 'You did your thing - now I've got to do mine.' After he gave his speech and had gone through all of the scheduled activity, Dad relaxed considerably. He had made it. At 94 and 95 years of age, he had taken major trips, been involved with interviews for my book, *Power and Gender*, and gave a speech before a crowd of about 100. As we sat in the Washington airport on the way back from our first trip, he said, 'I never in my wildest dreams, thought you would write a book. I am proud.'

"Once home in Cedar Falls, Dad appeared introspective. I recall vividly, one afternoon as he sat in a chair with its back to our large picture window. He spoke softly, 'All this time, I now know why I have lived so long. I know what your mother needed,' he waved his left hand as to dismiss his next sentence. 'God rest her soul,' his voice dropped even lower as he recognized the finality of death and of time. 'We are only given so many years -- on this earth.' He again waved his hand. My father possesses a truly positive and forward looking attitude toward life. He looks back only to reminisce or to learn. He continues his desire to learn in the sunset of his life, and that never ceases to amaze me. The purpose of his learning is always to further his service to his family, friends, church, and society."

Whenever I could, I went to Mason City to see Clarence Leffelbein. Clarence was born June 30, 1912

Chapter 10 - 1990-1999

in Dawson, Nebraska. Clarence's mother, Mattie and Marie's mother, Rosa, were sisters. When Clarence's wife was alive and the kids were still at home, they'd come down here a couple three times a year and we'd go up there. I always kind of liked him. He was a slow, easy going guy. He never did anything but farm. The only place he'd ever go was to church. As he got older, he was crippled up with arthritis. It would take him five minutes to go from one room to the next. He lived alone on his farm outside Mason City. Clarence had a great deal of foresight when he sold his farm many years before. He retained the right to use the house and buildings as long as he wanted. He never gave up his positive outlook on life or his faith.

Clarence died September 18, 1996. Funeral services were September 23, 1996. My nephew, Bill Kuehner, his wife, Carolyn, and I drove to Lexington, Nebraska for the funeral. As Bill tells it, "After the service, we attended the burial service at the Stanley Cemetery, a rural cemetery, quite isolated near the town of Amherst, Nebraska. After we left the cemetery, we drove on country roads to Ravenna, because this was the countryside that Warren knew while growing to adulthood."

Bill tells about an earlier time when he and I had gone to see Clarence. "We drove up to the house on a dirt driveway overgrown with trees. Warren went to the door and hollered, 'Anyone home?' Clarence yelled back, 'Yea, come on in.' Clarence was in a wheelchair.

He suffered from rheumatoid arthritis, so he was quite limited in what he could do. We took old family pictures along for Clarence to identify. He had one small bulb over the kitchen table. He was able to identify nearly all of them. His eye sight was extremely good.

"Clarence had no air conditioning because he could not tolerate being cool due to his arthritis. He lived in three rooms of the house: kitchen, bathroom and living room. The remainder of the house was boarded off. His daughter from Lexington brought him food once a week and cleaned his house. The mailman looked in on him a couple times a week to make sure Clarence was O.K., and he took care of his cats.

"I'll never forget that day with Clarence. Here is this man in his 80s, disabled, living by himself, not asking for anything, while, the same day, in the Grand Island newspaper, I read of a woman in her prime of life who had cockroaches that had plugged up her stool. She blamed everyone for the mess that she herself had caused. Clarence, on the other hand, was an 80 year old man and he complained to no one and lived many miles from even a small town."

In the Spring of 1996, Ruby's enlarged heart kicked up too often. Ruby and I were not weary of heart, but we were more weary in body. Ruby couldn't walk but a few steps. She just couldn't get around anymore. On July 8, 1996, Ruby moved to a care facility. She didn't want to give up her place at Pletcher Terrace but she knew she had to.

Chapter 10 - 1990-1999

Over the years, I liked to call Rosemarie or send her items I came across that I liked. She always appreciated them. Rosemarie says, "The most touching message I ever received from my father arrived in the mail in February 1997. When I opened the mailed envelope, a penny and a peppermint candy came tumbling out. What, I remember thinking, is in here? As I examined the contents, I also found a rubber band, a tissue, a band-aid and a poem that my father had clipped from his church bulletin which read:

The Love Kit.

We give love and receive love in many ways. The items contained within are symbols to show you that someone cares about you.

1. A 'Rubber Band' to remind you of hugging and holding, those times when you wish to hold someone close to you.
2. A 'Piece of Candy' to remind you to spread sweetness wherever you may go.
3. A 'Tissue' to dry a tear in your neighbors eye.
4. A 'Band-Aid' for healing hurt feelings; your own or someone else's.
5. A 'Copper Penny' to remind you to share with others a-

round you.

With this love kit, he enclosed a brief greeting, 'I Love you. May God Bless, Dad.'

"On June 11, 1998, my birthday, as was his habit, my father telephoned early in the morning. 'Happy Birthday,' he said, 'Because I can't sing to you, I would like you to listen.' He played 'Happy Birthday to You.' It sounded like it was from a music box. This is my father, doing for others and finding ways to meaningfully remember others."

I like to volunteer. I did a lot of it at church. When I was 98, Pastor Russell wrote in the church newsletter, "At 98 years of age, Warren Keller is the most senior of our volunteers spotlighted this month. Warren has been a member of St. Pauls since 1936. As with all of our volunteers, he is not one to toot his own horn, however Warren has been involved in volunteering for 60 years. He explains, 'When we were children, we were on the (receiving) end and I felt empty.' By volunteering, Warren 'feels more content. It makes life most satisfying.' Warren would like to see people 'start (volunteering) a bit earlier than I did. They won't have so much to regret. You can't start too early!'"

In 1999, Fred Bosselman told Rosemarie, "I always admired Warren. He has always been a gentleman through the years, and that is a long time." And Nancy Kuehner said to Rosemarie, "As you write about Warren, I hope you capture his sharpness of mind."

Over the years, Howard and Colleen put some-

Chapter 10 - 1990-1999

thing in the paper when my birthday rolled around. In 1996, it was, "five-six pick-up sticks, Warren Keller turned 96." In 1997, it was, "who's 97 and a mighty fine feller? Why it could only be Warren Keller." In 1998, it was, "seven-eight lay them straight, Warren Keller turned 98." In 1999, Howard says, "We didn't have a jingle but we lined up a card shower."

When I turned 99, the pastor made a big deal of it in church. They sang happy birthday to me, and the pastor told everyone about Howard taking away my snow shovels. The church service is broadcast on the radio live. Howard says that the next day he had many folks comment about his taking my shovels away.

Rosemarie says, "Dad's birthday in 1999 was one of the most beautiful series of events that I have ever witnessed. Dad celebrated all month. On the second Tuesday of each month, the United Nebraska Bank has a lunch for senior citizens and gives a free meal for your birthday. St. Pauls Lutheran honored him with a lunch. On January 24, Pastor Russell told his nine o'clock congregation that Dad's 99th birthday was coming. He told a little about Dad's good life, and then invited Dad to stand up during the service so people could see him. The nine o'clock service was broadcasted on radio station KRGI AM. In St. Pauls Lutheran Church's January 25, 1999, newsletter, *The Epistle of St. Pauls*, Pastor Russell wrote a whole page about Dad. (See Appendix, "Pastor Russell's Paragraphs.)

Colleen and Howard Maxon organized another

card party in 1999, I received about 86 cards. I was asked why the small difference in number from 1995. I said, "My sister Clara's family, out in California had gotten all the kids and grand kids and great grand kids to each send me a card the last time-- that counted up."

As Rosemarie tells it, "On his birthday, January 29, the hometown newspaper, *The Grand Island Independent* featured Warren on the front page headlines,

major article with pictures. I will never forget the moment when we arrived that day from Cedar Falls. Dad was sitting on the sofa waiting for us. The newspaper lay folded by his side. 'Dad,' I gleefully acknowledged, 'Not many people get on the main article of the front page of a newspaper.' Humbly, he smiled. The same article and head shot was featured on *The Independent's* Web Site. 'Turnin' 99 in '99: Islander still going strong as he nears century mark.'[1]

"When my eyes first rested on the picture of my Daddy's hands, I thought of the song, 'Daddy's Hands.' 'Daddy's hands held my mother tight and were soft and kind when I

cried.' And, true to the song, you can 'read quite a story in the callouses and lines' because they are the mark of "years of work and worry." Now, at the sunset of his life, his hands are folded prayerfully, and I am left with the thoughts of the song's final verse, 'If I could do things over, I'd live my life again. And never take for granted the love in daddy's hands.'"[2]

Howard says, "In the evening, when I would be out to my driveway, I could see Warren sitting at the kitchen table eating or writing. One time, I saw him with his head bowed and hands together in prayer. I thought, the trick to a long good life is to be close to your God."

ENDNOTES

1. news@theIndependent.com," Friday, January 29, 1999. Internet. Online. Available: http://www.theindependent.com/Archive/, Feb. 5, 1999.

2. Available: Dave Olson, "Cowpie Bunkhouse," Submissions, May 9, 1996. Internet. Online. Available: http://www.roughstock.com/cowpie/cowpie-songs/d/dunn_holly/daddys_hands.crd., Mar. 6, 1999.

Appendix

Harvey and Rose Keller's Marriage Record
April 2, 1894

A Man of the Twentieth Century

Warren and Marie's Wedding License
December 23, 1926

This Certifies

That on the 23 day of December in the year of our Lord One Thousand Nine Hundred Twenty Six at Grand Island, Nebr. Mr. Warren Valorous Keller of Grand Island and Miss Marie Wilhelmina Kuehner of Douphan, Nebr.

WERE BY ME UNITED IN

Holy Matrimony

According to the ordinance of God and the Laws of The State of Nebraska

Witnesses:
Mrs. Richard Kuehner
Wm Kuehner

J. H. Mullin
County Judge
Officiating

What therefore God hath joined together
Let no man put asunder St. Mathew 19:6

Appendix

Warren Keller's Baptismal Certificate, St. Pauls Lutheran Church, April 5, 1936

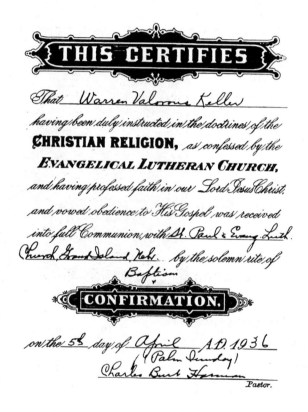

A Man of the Twentieth Century

Front Page Story on Warren Keller,
Grand Island *Independent*, January 29, 1999

Turnin' 99 in '99

Islander still going strong as he nears century mark

By Carol Bryant
The *Independent* [1]

Independent/Gerik Parmele

Warren Keller is 99 today.

About five years ago, former neighbor Howard Maxon took Keller's snow shovel so he wouldn't scoop his walks.

Keller bought a snowblower.

Another time, Maxon discovered that Keller was on his roof. After Keller came down, the city/county emergency management director took his ladder. Maxon lived next door to Keller of 412 W. 16th from 1985 to 1996.

Although he will turn 99 today, Warren Keller still keeps active in church activities and visiting friends.

"Our life has been enhanced by knowing him," Maxon said. "He is a swell fellow. He is such a positive influence on so many people. ... He's in really good shape."

Keller still drives, too. He said he stays away from interstate driving and doesn't drive at night.

Most afternoons, he drives his Ford Taurus to Wedgewood Nursing Home, where he visits his "lady friend," Ruby Loop.

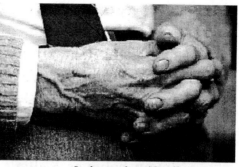
Independent/Gerik Parmele

Friends say Keller's good health comes from working as a meter reader.

"If you look real close, you'll see a sparkle in their eyes," Maxon said.

Keller's wife, Marie, died from leukemia in 1979. His son died from emphysema. His daughter, Rosemarie Skaine, lives in Cedar Falls, Iowa.

On Wednesday, Keller attended Bible study at St. Pauls Lutheran Church and stayed for the noon senior citizens meal. Then he headed to Wedgewood to see Loop.

John Russell, senior pastor at St. Pauls, said Keller attended church 51 times during 1998, which included services during the week. Keller joined the church in 1936.

He usually attends the 5 p.m. Saturday service but goes to the 9 a.m. Sunday service in the winter to avoid driving at night. Several years ago, Keller had perfect attendance in a two-year Bible study.

Three years ago, Keller signed up for nine months of Stephen Ministry training, Russell said. Another time, he phoned Russell and set up an appointment. Keller told the minister he wanted to do something to help others and wrote a $1,000 check to help finance a summer youth group trip.

"He doesn't think about himself," Russell said.

Maxon believes Keller's years as a city electric meter reader have contributed to his long life.

"He owes his good health to all that fresh air and exercise he got," Maxon said.

"I'll never forget the first time I met him," Maxon said. Keller was standing in his driveway, leaning on his car

"I greeted him. He says, 'Keller's the name. Warren.' He was a wonderful neighbor," Maxon said.

He took away Keller's shovels after Keller shoveled his own walks and those for two neighbors, then collapsed and ended up in St. Francis Medical Center's intensive care unit. Keller said his heart had stopped, but doctors revived him.

Keller talked about his life Wednesday afternoon during one of his regular visits at Wedgewood. He wore a white long-sleeved shirt, maroon tie, gray sweater and gray pants.

Keller was born in a sod house in Mason City. The roof leaked whenever it rained, and beds rested on

Appendix

boards so they wouldn't sink into the ground. The closest water supply was 100 feet from their home.

He had five sisters and one brother.

"My family's all gone," he said.

Keller described the first church he attended as an old sod chicken house.

"We didn't have any preacher," he said.

"I was 8 years old before I ever saw a car. I rode in the first car I ever saw," he said.

He moved to Grand Island in 1924 and began working for the city in 1925. His initial wage was 35 cents an hour. Loop's late husband was his first supervisor.

"Ever since 1980, we've been eating dinner together," Keller said about Loop.

He worked for the city until May 8, 1965, when "the federal government made me quit." He worked for Commercial National Bank until he was 83, then retired for good.

Keller said he has no explanation for his long life.

"The Lord takes care of that. Maybe he doesn't want me up there yet. I eat what I want to," he said. "I just live a day at a time. That's the way I've always lived."

Keller cooks most of his meals but likes to eat out.

"I like old-fashioned cooking -- meat, potatoes and bread," he said.

He'll eat a birthday meal at the home of his wife's nephew, Dick Kuehner of Phillips.

Maxon said he's not sure Keller will be "Y2K" compliant.

Keller has a different view of the year 2000.

"It's just another year to me."

Pastor Russell's Paragraphs[2]

I have been reflecting over the past couple of days about what makes some people positive and forward looking in a world where so many people can be negative and critical. What prompted my reflecting was one individual. We sang happy birthday to him at the 9: o'clock service last Sunday --- Warren Keller who will be 99 this week. He is a remarkable person.

About five years ago he ended up in Intensive Care at St. Francis after shoveling snow in his driveway. When it became clear that he would recover, he received a stern lecture from me about not doing something dumb like that again! His next door neighbor at the time, Howard Maxon, took his shovel to his own house so it would not happen again. The next fall he came out of church one Saturday night and told me I didn't need to worry about him shoveling snow. He had bought a big snow blower. Now he not only does his own driveway but his neighbor's as well.

Then, three years ago he signed up for Stephen Ministry training. The training is nine months long. He started it at age 96! How many people that age would take on a nine month project? What a positive outlook.

Most recently Howard Maxon went over to see him and discovered him up on the roof of his house. Warren was concerned that the eave troughs might collapse from the weight of the ice in them. This time Howard took his ladder home with him after he got Warren off the roof.

Do not ever go over to see him in the afternoon. He is never there. That is when he drives his own car to Wedgewood to help the "old people." He can be found pushing people around in their wheelchairs and visiting with people, including his long time "girl friend" as he calls her.

A couple of years ago he phoned and wanted to come and see me. He came to the office and told me that the Lord had been so good to him that he wanted to do something to help others. We talked about the summer youth trip. He asked me to write out a check for $1,000 and he would sign it. Then he was on his way to do something else.

As active and busy as he is, worship is a top priority. In 1998, at age 98, he was at worship 51 times. During the winter he comes on Sunday morning. When the days are longer he is always at the Saturday evening service. Few of our members are as regular at worship as he is. Talk about faithfulness and having one's priorities clear.

Being as active as he is at age 99 obviously has something to do with genes. That is for sure. But there has to be more to it than that, much more. Attitude is crucial.

As I have known him over these past fifteen years, the one thing that comes through so very clear is his sense of servanthood. His thoughts are outward toward other people. That is reflected in his gift to youth and his visits to Wedgewood. It is also the spirit of doing and not depending upon other people --- be it the snow on the driveway or the ice in the eave troughs.

Whenever the temptation arises to turn in on yourself, to fell sorry for yourself, to wonder what others have done for you lately, stop and think about Warren. In a very quiet way he reflects the Christian faith in his daily living and I suspect it is that deep, quiet faith that is lived out every day that has been a major contributor to his very long life.

ENDNOTES

1. news@theIndependent.com," Friday, January 29, 1999. Internet. Online. Available: http://www.theindependent.com/Archive/, Feb. 5, 1999.

2. "Pastor Russell's Paragraphs," *The Epistle of St. Pauls*, St Pauls Lutheran Church, Jan. 25, 1999, 10:2, 4.

Index

A
A Man from Worms vi-vii
airplanes 49-50
Alps 2
Alliance, NE 24
Allied Contractors 26
Amherst, NE 109
Amsbarry, Burt 8
Amsberry, Becky 7
Amsberry, Francis Everett 1
Amsberry, Jess 7
Amsberry, Lucy Beard 1, 91
Amsberry, William 1
Amsberry (Amsbary), William A. 6
Anderson, Dr. 88
Anderson, Nels 7
Ansley, NE 26
Arendt, William F. vi-vii
Army Air Base (Air Field) 49-50
Army and Navy Club, Washington, D.C. 107-108
Ashland, NE 8

B
Baker, Dorothy Schoel vii
Basel, Switzerland 2
Bavaria 2
Beach-Shore Apartment Hotel 61
Bighorn Mountains 26
birthday card parties 106-107, 113-114
birthday 99 106-1-7, 112, Appendix 4
"Black Death" 2
Black Hills 26, 29, 41

blackouts (World War II) 52
Blue Mountains 53
Blue Ridge mountains 104
Bonneville Dam, OR 56
Bosselman Family & Friends Cookbook The vi-vii
Bosselman, Fred H. vi-vii,112
Bosselman, Maxine Forbes vi-vii
Boy Scouts 71
Brand, Irene107
Brand, Rod 107
bridge gang 25-27, 29-33
Broken Bow, NE 1, 27
Bryant, Carol 120
Buffalo, N.Y. 66, 67
bumming trip 23-26
Burdick, Clarence 37, 47-48, 74
Burlington train 7, 60
burro19
Butch (pet dog) 58

C
Cairo, NE vi-vii
Caldwell, Priscilla 18
Callaway, NE 27
Cameron, WY 53
Cannella, Dr. John J. 99
Capitol Theater 64
cars, Rambler 8, first saw 14, 19, 20, 22, Model T Ford 20, Reos 20, Ford Touring car 20, Overland 27, Model T Touring 30, Model T Roadster 34, Chevy Coupe (1932) 40-41, Ford (1941) 51, Chevrolet (1947) 61, 66, Ford (1954) 61, 69, Ford (1962) 73., V-8 Plymouth (1970) 81, Mercury (1980) 83, 85, 89, 90 Ford Taurus (1988) 90
Catalina Island 62
Cedar Falls, IA 75, 82-83, 85, 90-91, 97, 101-102, 105, 108, 114

Index

Chapman, NE 66
Cheyenne, WY 31, 53, 55
Chicago, IL 66
Christian Church, Grand Island 58
chuck wagon 25
Cincinnati, OH 105
City Utilities 33, Water 37-38, Electric 39-40, 63, Bill
    Collection 47-48, 49, 63, retirement 73, 75, 88
civil defense 52
Civil Rights Act 1964 71
Cleve, Alecia 5
Cloud Peak 25
Coleman, Ruby Roberts 6
Colorado Springs, CO 57
Columbia Gorge National Scenic Area 56
Columbia River, OR 54, 56
Coney Island 69
Commercial Bank 75-76, 77, 88
Cornell University (Ithaca, N.Y.) 68, 75
Cox, Joan vii
Coxen, Wayne 4, 22,

D
Dalles, The, OR 54
Davis, Albert 23, 24, 25
Dawson, NE 109
Densmore, Wallace 101-102
Denver, CO 62
Des Moines, IA 71, 97
Doniphan, NE vi, 5, 33-34
draft registration 26-27
dray wagon 13, 21
Drive-In Theater 64
Dubas, Monadine Schoel vii
dude ranch 25-26

E

Eagles (F.O.E.) 47
Eaton Brother's Dude Ranch 25-26
Edison, WA 8
Edwards, Frank 4
Elsbery, Ted 37
England 1
Epistle of St. Pauls 113
Evans, Margaret 4
Evanston, WY 61
Everett, Polly 1
Everett, Richard 1

F

Fairfield, Merle "Ping" 52
Falmlen, Nona 49
family xiii, 8-15
Feierfeil, Ray 58, 12
Flying G Ranch, Deckers, CO 66
Forest Lawn Cemetery, CA 62
Forst, Donald vii
Forst, Marceline Schoel vii
food cost 20-21, 50
Franzen, Richard 78, 88
Fremont, Darrell G. vii
funerals, early 1900s 15

G

garage, building 88-89
Garden of the Gods, CO 57
Gates, NE 26
genealogy 59
General Electric radio 52
Girl Scouts 59, 64-63, 66, 68-69
Glendale, CA 62

Index

Glovera Ballroom 41
Gockley, Don 49
Goehring, Elmer 58
Goehring, Lucille Sloggett vii, 57
Gordon, John E. "Ted" 107
Great Depression 39-40, 49
Grand Island, NE v, vi, vii, xi, xiii, xv, 4, 5, 21, 27, 31-39,
    75th Anniversary Celebration 39, entertainment 41-42,
    Senior High 57, 66, All-American City 67, Miss America
    67, centennial celebration 67, tornadoes 86
Grand Ol' Opry 38, 73
Green River, WY 29-30
Griffith's Park 62
Gooch's 13

H
Halloween 23
Harding, President 33
Hardman, Robert R. vii
Hastings, NE 62
Haymann, Arthur 57
Haymann, Ava 56-57
Hendrickson, Mrs. Elsie vii
Henry Keller Genealogy 2, 6
heart problems 88, 97-99, 101, 102, 110
heritage 1-6
Hermosa, SD 29
Hillsboro, OR 5. 52-55
History of the Descendants of John Hottel 6
Hitler 49
Holdredge, NE 65
Hood River, OR 56
Hot Springs, SD 29, 41,
Hottel, Barbara Anna 3, 4
Hottel, John 3

Hottel-Keller 103
Hottel-Keller reunion 1995 4, 107
Hottel Shield 2
horse 22, 45
Horsetail Falls, OR 56
house, 412 W. 15, 45-47. 51, 69, 120
housing, World War II 50
Hoyt, Mrs. 24
Hudnall, Nola 66

I
Independent The (Grand Island, NE) 57, 86-87, 91, 93, 96, 114, 115, 120, 121, 127
Indianapolis Speedway 105
Ithaca, NY 5, 68-69, 71, 75
Ithaca College 71

J
Japan 49
Jinks, Margaret Amsberry 1, 91
Jinks, Rose A. 1
Jinks, William Robert 1, 102
Johnson, Betty M. vii
Johnson, President Lyndon 71

K
Kaufman's store 42
Kear, V.A. 76
Kearney, NE vii, 41
Keller, Amos 2, 5
Keller, Blanche 3, 4, 8
Keller, Carin Little 5
Keller, Clara 3, 4
Keller, Emery 3, 4
Keller, Etna 3, 4, 8, 57, 60, 65-66

Index

Keller, George 3
Keller, Harvey S. 3, 4, 21, 52-56, 69, 117
Keller homestead 4, 103-105
Keller, Jacob 1
Keller, James 5
Keller, James (see also James Keller Skaine) 5, 71, 76, 82
Keller, Jane Weaver 3
Keller John M. 2
Keller Lorena 3, 4, 8, 22, 52
Keller, Marie W. Kuehner 5, 33-36, 39, 41-43, 46-47, 50-52, 58, 61-65, 67, 69, 72-74, 77-78, 80-81, 83, 85, 91, 109, 119, 122
Keller, Melissa 5
Keller, Rose 3, 4, 52, 7, 67, 117
Keller, Rosemarie xiii, 5, 43–45, 49, 52, 56, 58-69, 71-73, 78, 80-82, 85, 90-92, 97, 101-108, 111, 113-114, 121
Keller, Densmore, Twila 3, 4, 101-102
Keller, Warren V. v
    heritage 1-5, birth to 1910 7-16, church 15, 43, 76, 109, 111-113, 119-125, teen years 17-27, young adult 29-38, family life 39-63, retirement 71-76, working again 71-96, service 97-116, "Heritage, A Sketch in Pictures"91, baptism certificate 119, "Turnin' 99 in'99" 120
Keller, William H. 5, 39, 43-44, 47-49, 56-59, 65, 67, 69, 73, 76-78, 85-88, 91, 99
Kellogg's Krumble Bran cereal 59
Kemp, Wally 63-64
Kennedy, President John F. 71
King, Martin Luther 71
King's Ranch 24-25
Knottsberry Farm, CA 62
Kosh, Mr. and Mrs. Andy 74
Kramer, Robert v
Kuehner, Carolyn E. Guenther vi, 80, 109
Kuehner, Frieda 80-81

Kuehner Homestead 33-34, 80
Kuehner, Jennie Akerlund vi
Kuehner, Kaila K. vi
Kuehner, Kenda K. vi
Kuehner, Nancy L. vi, 112
Kuehner, Richard 42
Kuehner, Richard L. vi, 65, 78-80
Kuehner, Rosa Bosselman 35, 39, 43, 56, 63, 72, 109
Kuehner, William E. 35, 78-82
Kuehner II, William E. vi
Kuehner, William V. vi, 65, 78-80, 110

L
La Grande, OR 53
Labor Day 46-47
Lamb, Chester 17
Lamb, Leonard 25
Lamb, Leonard 17
Lamb, Leah 17
Lamb, Mabel 17
Lamb, Carey 17
Laramie, WY 31
Las Vegas, NV 61
Lawrence Welk band 41
Leffelbein, Clarence 109-110
Leffelbein, Mattie 109-110
Lexington, NE 109
Lincoln Land Company 7
Lincoln, NE 13, 19, 36, 40
Los Angeles, CA 61
Long Beach, CA 60-61
Lookout Mt., CA 62
Loop, Ruby Burnett Schoel v, vii, 36, 41, 85, 88, 91, 93-94,
    100-101, 111, 121
Love Kit 111-112

Index

Lutheran Hospital 81

M
Mason City, NE vii, xv, 1, 4, 7-16, 17-27, 32, 52, 102, 105, 109, 122
Mason, Honorable O.P. 1
Massachusetts Bay Colony 1
Maxon, Colleen vi, 89-90, 94, 97, 106, 112, 113
Maxon, Howard vi, 89-90, 92-95, 97-106, 112, 113, 115, 120, 125, 126
Maxon, John Howard vi, 95
Maxon, Luke Adrian vi
Maxon, Paul Andrew vi
Mayflower 1
McBride, Chuck 95
McBride, Mary 95
Medicine Bow, NE 30-31
Middle Tennessee State College 72
military police 49
Miller, Rosemary vii
Minneapolis, MN 66
Minstral Cathedral 2
Miss America 67
Mississippi River 66
Mitchellville, IA 71
Mohanna, Tim viii
Mohawk Lyric radio 38
Monongahela, PN 5
Morris Press vii
Mt. Hood 56
Mt. Olive, VA 4
Multnomah Falls, OR 56
Murfreesboro, TN 72-73

N
Nashville, TN 73
Nebraska Territory 8
Nebraska Veteran's Home 87
Nerdin, Stacey 62
New Amsterdam, IN 3, 102, 105
New Deal 40
New York City 69

O
Oakley, Allen 25
Obermeier, Jackie L. vi
Obermeier, Karla K. Kuehner vi
Obermeier, Tanner William vi
Oconto, NE 26
Ogallala, NE 6
Ohio River 105, 107
Old Livery Barn 19
Omaha, NE 26, 36, 60
Omaha World-Herald 57
opera house 23
Oswald, Lee Harvey 71
Ovid, N.Y. 69

P
Pacific Ocean 56, 61
Palatinate, Germany 2
Pearl Harbor 49
Penney's 47
pet dog 58
Peterson, Maggie 1-5
Peterson, Nikolai 1, I-9, 19, 102
Phelps, Frank 75
Philadelphia, PN 1, 2
Phillips, NE vi, 123

Index

Pikes Peak, CO 57
Pilgrims 1
Pletcher Terrace 101, 111
Plymouth 1
Portland, OR 52
Proffitt, Dr. 78, 88
Provo Mountains, UT 62

Q
Quaker Oat defense plant 51-52

R
radio Mohawk Lyric 38, stations 38, first 73
Rapid City, S.D. 29
rationing 50-51, 53
Rawlins, NE 31
Ravenna, NE 109
Record Printing Company vii, viii
Redwood tree 62
Redondo Beach 62
Reno, NV 62
Revolution 2
Reynolds, Debbie 64
Rhine 2
Rhodes, P.S. 2
Ritchie, Sharon (Miss America) 67
roads xv
Roberts, Lewis 4
Roberts, Uncle 14
Roosevelt, President Franklin D. 56
Roosevelt, President Teddy 36
Ruby, Jack 71
Rummery, Dr. 22
Rummery, Luther 21-22,
Runyan, Mrs. George 7

Rupp, I.D. 2
Russell, Pastor John v, xi-xii, 99-100, 112, 113, 121, 122, 125, 127

S
Sahalie Falls, OR 56
saloons and food 20-21
San Francisco Bay, CA 62
Sanders, Jim 58
Sargent, NE 26
Schoel, Bernelda Poehler vii
Schoel, Ercel vii
Schoel, Heine 36
school teacher 19
Schuyler, NE 60
Schwarzenacker, Bavaria 3
Seattle, WA 8
Seneca, NE 23
Sequoia National Park 62
Shenandoah County, Virginia 2
Shenandoah Iowa 41
Shenandoah Valley, Virginia 102, 103
Sheridan, WY 24, 26
Shumaker, Dr. E. S. 2, 6
Sherry, Eloise viii
Sioux Falls College, S.D. 66
Skaine, Camille Marie 5, 72, 73
Skaine, Forrest Todd viii, 5, 75-76
Skaine, James Cole xv-xvii, 5, 66-69, 71-72, 75, 85-86, 90, 91, 101, 102, 105, 107
Skaine, James Keller (*a.k.a.* James Keller) 5, 71, 5, 82
Skaine, James Taylor Jeremiah (T.J.) viii, 5
Skaine, Rosemarie Keller (see Rosemarie Keller)
Skaine, Ruth 67
Sloggett, Juan 4, 58
Sloggett, Lucille 57-58

Index

Sloggett, Wanda 57-58, 60
Sloggett, Wesley 58
Sloggett, Virginia 57-58
smallpox 23
sod house 7, 9, 11, 75-76, 122
Soldiers' Home 86
Sons and Daughters of the Soddies Inc. 76
Southside, W VA 1, 2, 3, 102, 105, 107
Statue of Liberty 69
St. Libory, NE 48
St. Pauls Lutheran Church v, viii, xi-xii, 43, 99, 113
St. Paul, NE 27
Stanley Cemetery 109
Steele, Donald 65
Stephen's Ministry, The viii
Stuart, Floyd 106
Stuhr Museum vii, 32-33
Sunset Blvd. 62
Switzerland 2

T
technology xv-xvi
television 77-78
Tell 2
Tom's Brook, VA 3, 103
trains 77
Twin Falls, ID 53

U
Union Pacific 32, 33, 37, 55, 56, 67-68
University Hospital, Omaha, NE 81
University of Northern Iowa 78, 86
University of South Dakota 68

V

Vermillion, S.D. 68
Veteran's Administration Hospital 87
Victrola 15
Viers Chapel Cemetery 1, 102, 105-106,
Vollnogle, Leslie A. vii

W

wages earlier get, 18, 10, 3-3, 9, 40,
Wahkeena Falls, OR 56
Washington, D.C. 103, 105
weather, drought 43-44, winter 44-45, 60, 63, 71,100 rain 63, hail 69, lightning 77-78, snow 63, tornadoes 86-87, frost 89
wedding, Rose and Harvey Keller 1, marriage record 117
wedding, Rosemarie and James Skaine 66-68
wedding, Warren and Marie 34-35, license 118, 50th anniversary 79-80
Wedgewood Care, xi, 121, 122, 126, 127
West Lawn Elementary School 49
Western Union 57
Whyte, John v, 92-93, 96-98
Whyte, Rosie v, 96-98
Wilson, Delbert 23, 24
Will Rogers' Station, CO 57
Williams, Duvall M. "Mac" Jr. 107
Wolfe Eye Clinic, Marshalltown, NE 90
Woodlief, Dr. 90
Woodstock, Virginia 2
Works Progress Administration (WPA) 40, 56
World War I21, 6, 11
World War II 49-53, 56
Worms, NE vi-vii, 48
Wymer's Hardware 21

Index

Z
Zweibrucken, Bavaria 3
Zwingli 2

About the Authors

Warren V. Keller was born in Mason City, Nebraska on January 29, 1900. He has lived all but a year and a half of his life in Nebraska. In his life, he experienced the technological and social changes that made the 20th Century, the American Century. He lives in Grand Island, Nebraska where he has lived since 1924.

Rosemarie Keller Skaine is Warren Keller's daughter. She is an author and has written two books. In 1996, *Power and Gender: Issues in Sexual Dominance and Harassment* was published. It received in 1997 The Gustavus Myers Center Award for the Study of Human Rights in North America. In 1999, *Women at War: Gender Issues of Americans in Combat* was published.

James C. Skaine is Warren Keller's son-in-law. He received his B.A. at Sioux Falls College, his M.A. at the University of South Dakota and did doctoral work at Cornell University and the University of Iowa. He is a retired professor of rhetoric and public address at the University of Northern Iowa.